Table of Contents

Part I

Apartheid's brilliance was its ability to persuade the vast majority of individuals to turn against one another. That is what it was, apart from hatred. You divide individuals into factions and incite animosity among them in order to govern them all.

Zulu, Xhosa, Tswana, Sotho, Venda, Ndebele, Tsonga, Pedi, and other tribes were divided into distinct languages, despite the fact that black South Africans outnumbered European South Africans by nearly five to one at the time. These tribal factions engaged in conflict and warfare for an extended period of time prior to the establishment of apartheid. Then, the white rule utilized this animosity to divide and conquer. All nonwhite individuals were systematically categorized into a variety of categories and subgroups. Subsequently, these organizations were granted varying degrees of rights and privileges in order to maintain their opposition.

The Zulu and Xhosa, South Africa's two dominant tribes, were perhaps the most starkly divided. The Zulu guy is referred to as the warrior. He is filled with pride. He fights with his head bowed. When the colonial armies invaded, the Zulu rushed into battle with spears and shields, facing off against men armed with guns. Despite the fact that the Zulu were massacred by the thousands, they continued to engage in combat. Conversely, the Xhosa take pride in their identity as intellectuals. My mother is of Xhosa descent. Nelson Mandela was of Xhosa descent. The Xhosa also engaged in a protracted conflict with the white man; however, several Xhosa chiefs adopted a more agile strategy after witnessing the futility of combat against a more well-equipped adversary. "These white individuals are present regardless of our preferences," they declared. "Let us investigate the resources they have that could be beneficial to us." We should master English rather than being resistant to it. We will be able to comprehend the white man's statements and compel him to engage in negotiations with us.

The Zulu engaged in a conflict with the white man. The white male and the Xhosa engaged in a game of chess. Both were unsuccessful for an extended period, and they each held the other accountable for a problem that neither had initiated. The bitterness persisted. A common adversary maintained the control over those emotions for decades. Subsequently, apartheid was abolished, Mandela was granted freedom, and black South Africa engaged in a civil conflict with itself.

Trevor Noah

Biography

THE UNTOLD STORIES OF TREVOR NOAH'S CHILDHOOD

Chapter 1: Run

Occasionally, in major Hollywood films, there are exhilarating chase sequences in which an individual is thrown from a moving vehicle or jumps. The individual falls to the ground and rolls for a brief period. They then come to a halt, emerge, and dust themselves off as if it were no big thing. Whenever I encounter that, I think, "That is utter nonsense." The impact of being ejected from a moving vehicle is significantly more painful.

My mother tossed me from a moving vehicle when I was nine years old. It transpired on a Sunday. I am aware that it occurred on a Sunday because we were returning from church, and in my childhood, Sundays were reserved for worship. We never failed to attend worship. My mother was and remains a profoundly religious woman. Extremely Christian. The religion of our colonizers was adopted by black South Africans, as was the case with indigenous peoples worldwide. The term "adopt" refers to the fact that it was imposed upon us. The native was treated with considerable severity by the European man. "You must pray to Jesus," he advised. "You will be saved by Jesus." The native responded, "Well, we do require saving—from you, but that is irrelevant." Therefore, we should attempt to investigate this Jesus phenomenon.

My family is religious as a whole; however, my grandma, who was raised in the traditional Xhosa culture, maintained a balance between her Christian faith and the traditional beliefs of her people. She communicated with the spirits of our ancestors. My mother was a staunch supporter of Jesus. I was perplexed for an extended period of time as to why so many black individuals had renounced their indigenous faith in favor of Christianity. However, the longer I sat in those pews and the more we attended church, the more I was able to understand the workings of Christianity: If you are a Native American and you pray to the coyotes, you are considered a savage. If you are African and pray to your progenitors, you are considered a primitive. However, it is only common sense that white individuals pray to a man who can transform water into wine.

Church, or some form of church, was a part of my childhood on at least four evenings per week. The prayer meeting was held on Tuesday evening. Bible study was conducted on Wednesday evening. Youth worship was held on Thursday evening. We were granted time off on

Friday and Saturday. (It is now time to commit sin!) Afterward, we attended church on Sunday. To be precise, there are three temples. One of the reasons we visited three churches was that my mother claimed that each one provided her with a unique experience. The initial congregation sang songs of joy in honor of the Lord. My mother was particularly fond of the second church, as it provided a comprehensive examination of the scripture. The third church was a place where the Holy Spirit was genuinely felt, offering catharsis and passion. I observed that each church had a unique ethnic composition as we alternated between them, entirely by chance: It was a mixed congregation known as Jubilant congregation. The analytical church was a white church. The black church was a cathartic, impassioned church.

Rhema Bible parish was a mixed parish. Rhema was one of those suburban megachurches that were enormous and ultramodern. Ray McCauley, the pastor, was an ex-bodybuilder with the demeanor of a cheerleader and a broad smile. Pastor Ray had participated in the 1974 Mr. Universe competition. He took third position. Arnold Schwarzenegger emerged victorious that year. Ray would be onstage every week, exerting himself to portray Jesus as suave. Arena-style seating was available, and a rock band performed the most recent Christian contemporary pop as they jammed. Everyone participated in the singing, and it was permissible to sing along without understanding the lyrics, as they were displayed on the Jumbotron. In essence, it was Christian cabaret. I have consistently loved attending diverse churches.

Rosebank Union was a white church located in Sandton, a posh and predominantly white area of Johannesburg. The fact that I was exempt from attending the main service made white church my favorite. We read several interesting stories in Sunday school.

I was exposed to very little popular culture growing up. My mother's home was off-limits to Boyz II Men. Songs about a guy who spends the entire night groping a girl? No, no, no. That was prohibited. I wouldn't know what was going on when I heard the other students at school singing "End of the Road." Although I was aware of the Boyz II Men, I was not really sure who they were. I was solely familiar with church music, which consisted of uplifting, soaring tunes that extolled Jesus. The same applied to movies. My mother didn't want violent and sexy films to contaminate my head. Thus, the Bible served as my action film. My superhero was Samson. A man using a donkey's jawbone to beat a thousand people to death? That is really awesome. The storyline eventually wanes when Paul starts writing letters to the Ephesians, but what about the Old Testament and the Gospels? Anything from those pages, chapters, and verses might be quoted by me. I kicked everyone's ass during the weekly Bible games and quizzes at White Church.

The Black Church came next. We attempted every black church service that was happening, which was always going on somewhere. That usually meant a tent revival-style outdoor church in the township. My grandmother's church was an old-fashioned Methodist congregation with five hundred African grandmothers wearing blue-and-white blouses, holding their Bibles and patiently burning in the scorching African heat. That's where we generally attended. I won't lie, black church was difficult. No air conditioning. Jumbotrons don't have lyrics. I was perplexed since white church was just about an hour long—in and out, thanks for coming—but it went on forever, for at least three or four hours. However, I would spend what seemed like an eternity sitting at Black Church, trying to understand why time passed so slowly. Does time really have the ability to stop? In that case, why does it end at the Black church but not the White one? Black people suffered more than white people, so I finally came to the conclusion that we needed more time with Jesus. My mother used to remark, "I'm here to fill up on my blessings for the week." She believed that we accumulated more blessings, such as a Starbucks Rewards Card, the more time we spent at church.

There was one redeeming grace for the Black Church. I would get to see the preacher cast devils out of people if I could stay until the third or fourth hour. Demon-possessed people would begin to run like madmen up and down the aisles, screaming in tongues. Like club bouncers, the ushers would tackle them and keep them down for the pastor. "I cast out this spirit in the name of Jesus!" the preacher would yell as he grabbed their heads and forcibly shook them back and forth. While some pastors were more aggressive than others, they all persisted until the demon was vanquished and the congregation had gone limp and slumped on the platform. Someone has to go down. Since the demon was strong if he didn't fall, the pastor had to attack him even more forcefully. You might play in the NFL as a linebacker. didn't matter. You were being taken down by that pastor. Oh my, that was enjoyable.

Like all Sundays, this one began as usual—the Sunday I was flung from a moving car. My mother prepared me porridge for breakfast after waking me up. While she dressed my nine-month-old baby brother Andrew, I took a bath. We then proceeded to the driveway, but the car wouldn't start when we were all buckled up and prepared to leave. My mother bought this old, dilapidated, bright-tangerine Volkswagen Beetle for almost nothing. It was always breaking down, which is why she acquired it for almost nothing. I still detest used automobiles. Almost every negative event in my life can be linked to a used automobile. I received punishment for being late to school because of used autos. We were abandoned hitchhiking on the side of the expressway by used automobiles. My mom also got married because of a used automobile.

Even though I was a huge churchgoer, the thought of a nine-hour commute—from mixed to white to black to white to white again—was simply too much to bear. Using public transportation would be twice as difficult and time-consuming as driving, which was already a terrible experience. I prayed in my mind, "Please say we'll just stay home," when the Volkswagen wouldn't start. Say we'll simply stay at home, please. I knew I had a hard day ahead of me when I looked over and saw my mother's determined expression with her jaw set.

"Come," she said. "We intend to capture minibuses."

——

In addition to being religious, my mother is also obstinate. That's it once she makes up her mind. In fact, setbacks that would typically cause someone to alter their plans, such as a car breaking down, simply strengthened her resolve to keep going.

Regarding the halted car, she declared, "It's the Devil." "Going to church is something that the Devil opposes. We must therefore catch busses.

Every time I encountered my mother's religious intransigence, I made an effort to politely respond with a different viewpoint.

"Alternatively," I replied, "the Lord knows that we shouldn't be going to church today, so he made sure the car wouldn't start so that we could stay home as a family and take a day off, because even the Lord took a nap."

"Oh, Trevor, that's the Devil speaking."

"No, because Jesus is in charge. If Jesus were in charge and we prayed to him, he would have allowed the car to start, but he hasn't, so—"

"No, Trevor! Jesus occasionally places challenges in your path to test your ability to overcome them. similar to Job. It might be a test.

"Oh! Indeed, mother. However, the test can be to see if we can accept what has happened, remain at home, and give thanks to Jesus for his wisdom.

"No. The Devil is speaking there. Go change your clothes now.

"But, Mom!"

"Hey Trevor! "Sun'qhela!"

The term "sun'qhela" has multiple meanings. It says "just try me," "don't underestimate me," and "don't undermine me." It is simultaneously a threat and a command. Xhosa parents frequently say that to their children. Every time I heard it, I knew that the conversation was finished and that I would be given a spanking, or hiding, if I said anything else.

I was a student at Maryvale College, a private Catholic school at the time. Every year I won the Maryvale Sports Day championship, and every year my mother took home the Moms' Trophy. Why? Because I was constantly fleeing to avoid getting kicked in the ass while she was constantly chasing me to do so. No one ran like my mother and me. She wasn't one of those mothers that would come over here and hide. She would give it to you for free. She was also a thrower. You were being attacked by whatever was beside her. I had to catch it and set it down if it was breakable. The ass-kicking would be even worse if it broke, and I would also be at fault. I would have to catch the vase she flung at me, set it down, and then go. I would have to ask myself, "Is it valuable?" in a moment. Indeed. Is it brittle? Indeed. Grab it, set it down, and then sprint.

My mom and I had a really Tom and Jerry relationship. I was mischievous; she was the harsh disciplinarian. I would use the change from the milk and bread to play arcade games in the supermarket, so I wouldn't return home soon away when she sent me out to get groceries. I was a huge videogame fan. I could go on and on about one play. Time would pass quickly after I tossed a coin, and then I would see a woman wearing a belt behind me. It was a race. I would bolt out the door and make my way through Eden Park's dusty streets, climbing over walls and squeezing through backyards. Everyone was aware that Trevor's mother would be close behind him when his child came through like a tiger. She had the ability to run at full speed in high heels, but if she truly wanted to pursue me, she would kick off her shoes and continue to run at full speed. Her heels would go flying when she made this strange ankle maneuver, and she wouldn't even skip a step. I realized then that she was now in turbo mode.

She always caught me when I was younger, but as I grew older, I became faster, and when speed wasn't enough, she would employ cunning. She would shout, "Stop! Thief!" whenever I tried to flee. She would treat her own child in this way. Unless it's mob justice, in which case everyone wants to be involved, no one in South Africa gets involved in other people's affairs. She would shout, "Thief!" knowing that it would turn the entire neighborhood against me. Then, strangers would try to grab me and tackle me, and I would have to evade them while yelling, "I'm not a thief! I am her son.

The last thing I wanted to do on Sunday morning was board a congested minibus. However, the moment my mother uttered the word "sun'qhela," I knew my fate was sealed. Andrew was collected by her, and we exited the Volkswagen to attempt to secure a transport.

The day Nelson Mandela was liberated from prison, I was five years old, or nearly six. I recall witnessing it on television, and everyone was ecstatic. I was unaware of the reason for our happiness; it was simply the case. I was cognizant of the fact that apartheid was on the brink of its demise, which was a significant event; however, I was unable to comprehend the complexities of the situation.

What I do recall, and what I will never forget, is the violence that ensued. The Bloodless Revolution is a term that occasionally refers to the victory of democracy over apartheid. It is so named due to the minimal amount of white blood that was shed. In the streets, black blood flowed.

We were aware that the black man would now be in power as the apartheid regime collapsed. The query was, "Which black man?" Violence ensued between the African National Congress (ANC) and the Inkatha Freedom Party as they vied for power. The political dynamic between these two groups was intricate; however, the most straightforward interpretation is as a proxy conflict between the Zulu and Xhosa. The Inkatha were primarily Zulu, highly nationalistic, and militant. The African National Congress (ANC) was a coalition that encompassed a variety of tribes; however, its leaders were predominantly Xhosa at the time. Rather than collaborating to achieve peace, they turned on one another, perpetrating acts of unspeakable brutality. Riots of a significant scale ensued. Thousands of individuals were slain. Necklacing was prevalent. This is the location where individuals would restrain an individual and place a rubber tire over their torso, thereby pinning their limbs. They would then douse him with gasoline, set him ablaze, and immolate him. Inkatha was victimized by the ANC. Inkatha perpetrated this act against the ANC as well. One day, while en route to school, I observed one of those charred corpses on the side of the road. In the evenings, my mother and I would activate our diminutive black-and-white television and observe the news. Twelve individuals were fatally injured. Fifty individuals were slain. One hundred individuals were slain.

The extensive townships of the East Rand, Thokoza, and Katlehong, which were the sites of some of the most horrific Inkatha–ANC clashes, were not far from Eden Park. The neighborhood would be on fire at least once a month when we would drive home. The thoroughfare was occupied by hundreds of rioters. My mother would carefully navigate the car through the masses and around blockades constructed from flaming tires. "Nothing burns like a tire; it rages with a fury that is beyond comprehension." We experienced the sensation of being trapped within an oven as we drove past the smoldering blockades. I used to tell my mother, "I believe Satan burns tires in Hell."

All of our neighbors would prudently shelter behind closed doors whenever the rioting erupted. However, my mother is not included. She would proceed directly to the exit, and as we made our way past the blockades, she would offer the protestors this expression. Permit me to proceed. I am not involved in this matter. Her resolve was unyielding in the presence of peril. I was consistently astounded by that. The presence of a conflict on our doorstep was irrelevant. She had obligations and destinations to attend. She continued to attend church despite the fact that her vehicle was malfunctioning due to her intransigence. If there were five hundred rioters with a blockade of smoldering tires on the main road out of Eden Park, my mother would instruct me to "Get dressed." I am required to report to work. It is imperative that you attend education.

"However, are you not apprehensive?" I would say. "There is only one of you, and there are a multitude of them."

She would say, "My dear, I am not alone." "I have the support of all the angels of Heaven."

I would reply, "It would be beneficial if we could observe them." "Because I am under the impression that the rioters are unaware of their presence."

She would assure me that there was no need for concern. She consistently returned to the maxim that guided her life: "If God is with me, who can be against me?" She was never frightened. Despite the fact that she was supposed to be.

On that Sunday without a car, we visited a number of churches before arriving at White Church as per normal. It was dark and we were by ourselves when we left Rosebank Union. I was worn out from the nonstop minibus rides from mixed churches to black churches to white churches. At least nine o'clock had arrived. You didn't want to be out so late at night during those times because of the rioting and violence that were occurring. There were no minibuses when we were at the intersection of Oxford Road and Jellicoe Avenue, in the center of Johannesburg's affluent, white suburbs. The streets were deserted.

I really wanted to convey to my mother, "You see? God intended for us to remain at home for this reason. However, after seeing the look on her face, I refrained from speaking. This was not one of those occasions when I could smack my mother.

We kept waiting for a minibus to pass. White folks still wanted us to come wipe their floors and clean their restrooms during apartheid, even though the government did not provide public transit for Black people. Black people developed their own transit system, an unofficial bus route network run by private associations that operated completely outside the law, because necessity is the mother of invention. The minibus industry was essentially organized crime as it was totally uncontrolled. They would quarrel over who controlled what, and different groups took different routes. There was a lot of violence, bribery, and overall shadiness, as well as a lot of money paid for protection from violence. Stealing a route from a competing group was the one thing you didn't do. Route thieves would be put to death. Minibuses were likewise highly unreliable due to their lack of regulation. They arrived when they did. They didn't when they didn't.

As I stood outside Rosebank Union, I was literally nodding off. No sign of a minibus. "Let's hitchhike," my mother finally said. After what seemed like an eternity of walking, a car pulled up and stopped. We accepted the driver's offer of a ride. A minibus abruptly veered directly in front of the automobile and stopped us before we had gone five feet.

An iwisa, a big, traditional Zulu weapon—basically, a war club—was carried out by a Zulu driver. People's skulls are smashed into them. His comrade, another man, exited the passenger side. The man who had offered us a ride was grabbed by them as they approached the driver's side of the car, dragged him out, and began slapping their clubs in his face. "Why are you robbing our clients? You're picking them up, but why?

They appeared to be planning to murder this man. I was aware that occasionally that occurred. My mother raised her voice. "Listen, he was only assisting me. Get away from him. We'll accompany you. That's what we originally desired. Thus, we exited the first vehicle and boarded the minibus.

The van was empty except for us. Not only are South African minibus drivers vicious thugs, but they are also known for their constant whining and arguing with passengers. This driver was quite irate. He began lecturing my mother about being in a car with a man who wasn't her husband as we were driving. There were no strange men lecturing my mother. He became very agitated when he heard her conversing in Xhosa and she urged him to mind his own business. Stereotypes about Xhosa and Zulu women were just as deeply embedded as those about males. Zulu women were obedient and well-behaved. Xhosa women were disloyal and promiscuous. His tribe opponent, my mother, was a Xhosa woman with two young children, one of them was mixed, and she was by herself. A whore who sleeps with white males, not just a whore. He said, "Oh, you're a Xhosa." That clarifies it. getting into the cars of strangers. A repulsive woman.

He was ranting at her from the front seat, calling her names, waving his finger in the rearview mirror, and becoming increasingly threatening as my mom reprimanded him. Eventually, he remarked, "That's the problem with you Xhosa women." You're all sluts, and you're going to get your lesson tonight.

He drove away. He slowed down to check for traffic at junctions before accelerating past them, but he wasn't stopping. In those days, death was never far away. My mother could have been raped at that point. We might be killed. All of these were good choices. I was so exhausted that I simply wanted to go to sleep, so I didn't really understand the danger we were in at the time. My mother also maintained her composure. I didn't know to panic since she didn't. She simply persisted in attempting to reason with him.

"Bhuti, I apologize if we have offended you. Just let us out here, please—

"No."

It's okay, really. We can simply stroll—" "No."

He sped down Oxford Road, with no other vehicles in the lanes. I was seated closest to the sliding door of the minibus. My mom held baby Andrew when she sat behind me. "Trevor, when he slows down at the next intersection, I'm going to open the door and we're going to jump," she murmured to me as she peered out the window at the passing road.

By that time, I had fallen asleep entirely, so I didn't hear a word she said. The driver reduced the speed a little to inspect the road and look around when we reached the next traffic signal. Pulling the sliding door open, my mother grabbed me and tossed me as far out as she could. Then she grabbed Andrew, rolled into a ball, and jumped out behind me.

Before the agony struck, everything seemed like a dream. Bam! I gave the pavement a strong whack. We crashed and tumbled and rolled and rolled as my mother landed directly next to me. Now I was really awake. I woke up half sleeping and thought, "What the hell?" I eventually stopped and got to my feet, totally lost. My mother was already up as I turned to look around. She shouted as she turned to face me.

"Go!"

I ran, she ran, and no one ran as much as my mother and I did.

I just knew what to do, which is strange to explain. It was innate, acquired in a society where violence was constantly present and ready to explode. I knew to run for shelter when the police stormed into the townships with their armored cars, helicopters, and riot gear. Get away and hide. Even at age five, I was aware of that. I could have been unfazed by being flung from a speeding minibus if my circumstances had been different. I would have stood there like a fool and asked, "Mom, what's going on? Why do my legs hurt so much? However, none of that was present. I fled when Mom said to. I fled like a gazelle fleeing a lion.

The males attempted to pursue us after stopping the minibus and getting off, but they were unsuccessful. We smoked them. They were probably shocked. I can still see the expression of complete confusion on their faces as I looked back and watched them give up. What just took place? Who would have guessed that a mother with two young children could run that quickly? They were unaware that they were up against the Maryvale College sports day champions. When we finally reached a 24-hour gas station, we phoned the police and continued to drive. The men had long since left.

I had been running on adrenaline, and I still didn't understand why any of this had occurred. I became aware of my agony after we stopped jogging. I noticed that my arms' skin was ripped and scratched as I looked down. I was slashed and covered in blood. Mom was, too. But amazingly, my baby brother was fine. He had survived without any injuries after my mother had encircled him. Startled, I turned to face her.

"What was that? Why are we running?

"Why are we running?" What do you mean? The men were attempting to murder us.

"I never heard that from you! I was just thrown out of the automobile by you!

"Yes, I did tell you. How come you didn't jump?

"Leap! I was fast asleep!

"So I ought to have left you there so they could murder you?"

"Before they killed me, they would have at least woken me."

We went back and forth. I didn't grasp what had happened because I was too bewildered and upset at being thrown out of the automobile. My life had been rescued by my mother.

She responded, "Well, at least we're safe, thank God," as we recovered our breath and waited for the cops to arrive and take us home.

But I knew better at nine years old. This time, I wasn't going to remain silent.

"No, mother! God wasn't responsible for this! The Devil obviously deceived us into going out tonight, therefore you should have followed God's advice to stay inside when the car wouldn't start.

"No, Trevor! The Devil doesn't operate that way. This is a part of God's design, and He had a purpose if He wanted us here.

And we were back at it, debating what God would have us do. I exclaimed, "Look, Mom," at last. Although I am aware of your love for Jesus, you might invite him to our home the following week. since this evening wasn't enjoyable at all.

She smiled broadly and burst out laughing. We stood there, this small child and his mother, our arms and legs covered in blood and mud, laughing together through the pain in the middle of the night in the light of a gas station on the side of the road. I started laughing too.

Chapter 2: Born a Crime

I was reared in a mixed family in South Africa during apartheid, which was awkward in that I was the only mixed person in the family. The ethnicity of my mother, Patricia Nombuyiselo Noah, is African. The race of my father, Robert, is Caucasian. In particular, Swiss/Germans are invariably Swiss/German. While apartheid was in effect, engaging in sexual intercourse with an individual of a different ethnicity was considered one of the most severe offenses. It is unnecessary to mention that my parents were the perpetrators of that offense.

In a society that is founded on institutionalized racism, race-mixing not only challenges the system as unjust, but it also exposes it as unsustainable and incoherent. Race mixing demonstrates that races are capable of mingling and, in many instances, want to do so. Race-mixing is classified as a crime greater than treason due to the fact that a mixed individual exemplifies the opposite of the system's logic.

Breaking them resulted in a five-year penitentiary sentence. There were entire police squads whose sole responsibility was to peer through windows, an assignment that was evidently reserved for the most experienced law enforcement officers. If an interracial couple were to be apprehended, may God provide them with the necessary assistance. Individuals would be forcibly removed from the premises, subjected to physical assault, and ultimately apprehended by law enforcement. At least that is what they did to the black individual. In the case of the Caucasian individual, the message was more akin to, "Look, I will simply assert that you were inebriated; however, please refrain from repeating the behavior." I hope you have a wonderful day That is the case with a white male and a black woman. It would be fortunate for a black man to avoid being charged with rape if he were discovered having sex with a white woman.

If you inquire as to whether my mother ever contemplated the consequences of having a mixed child during apartheid, she will respond that she has not. She determined a method to accomplish her objective, and in the end, she executed it. It is necessary to possess a certain degree of fearlessness in order to confront an obstacle of the magnitude she did. If you pause to contemplate the consequences, you will never take action. Even so, it was an irrational and irresponsible decision. Our ability to evade detection for an extended period of time was contingent upon a multitude of favorable circumstances.

During the period of apartheid, black men were required to labor on farms, in factories, or in mines. A African woman was employed as a maid or in a factory. Your sole alternatives were essentially those. My mother was opposed to working in a factory. She was a subpar chef and would have been appalled by a white woman who dictated her daily activities. Thus, in accordance with her inherent disposition, she identified an alternative that was not among the alternatives that were presented to her: She enrolled in a typing course and a secretarial course. At that time, the process of a black woman learning to type was comparable to that of a blind individual learning to drive. Although it is commendable, it is improbable that you will ever be required to complete the assignment. Legally, white-collar and skilled-labor positions were exclusively designated for white individuals. Black individuals were not employed in offices. Nevertheless, my mother was a renegade, and she was fortunate in that her rebellion occurred at the appropriate time.

In an effort to pacify international protests regarding the atrocities and human rights violations of apartheid, the South African government implemented minor reforms in the early 1980s. The token hiring of black workers in low-level white-collar positions was one of the reforms. Similar to typists. She secured employment as a secretary at ICI, a multinational pharmaceutical company located in Braamfontein, a suburb of Johannesburg, through an employment agency.

My mother continued to reside with my grandmother in Soweto, the township to which my family had been relocated by the government decades prior, when she began working. However, my mother was dissatisfied with her home life and, at the age of twenty-two, she fled to reside in the heart of Johannesburg. There was only one issue: It was unlawful for black individuals to reside there.

In order to depart the township for employment in the city or for any other purpose, it was necessary to possess a pass that contained your ID number; failure to do so could result in arrest. Also, there was a curfew: Black individuals were required to return to their homes in the township by a specific hour or face detention. My mother did not show any concern. She was resolute in her resolve to never return home. Consequently, she resided in the city, concealing herself and sleeping in public lavatories until she acquired the necessary knowledge of the city's regulations from the other black women who had managed to establish themselves there: prostitutes.

Numerous prostitutes in the city were of Xhosa descent. They instructed my mother in survival skills and communicated in her native language. They instructed her on how to dress in a pair of maid's overalls in order to navigate the city without being stopped. Also, they introduced her to white men who were prepared to rent out flats in the city. Most of these men were foreigners, Germans, and Portuguese, who were unconcerned with the law and were content to sign a lease that provided a prostitute with a place to reside and work in exchange for a consistent income. My mother was not interested in any such arrangement; however, she was able to pay her rent due to her employment. She encountered a German individual through one of her prostitute acquaintances, and he consented to lease her a flat in his name. She relocated and acquired numerous maid's overalls to wear. She was apprehended on numerous occasions for failing to possess her identification card while traveling home from work and for being in a white area after hours. The penalty for violating the pass laws was either thirty days in prison or a fine of fifty rand, which was nearly half of her monthly salary. She would accumulate the funds, settle the penalty, and promptly resume her operations.

My mother's covert apartment was located in the Hillbrow district. Her address was 203. Robert, a tall, brown-haired, brown-eyed Swiss/German foreigner, was walking down the hallway. 206 was his residence. South Africa has always had a sizable expat population because it was formerly a trade colony. Here, people find their way. Many Germans. A lot of Dutch. At the time, Hillbrow was South Africa's Greenwich Village. It was a vibrant, liberal, and cosmopolitan scene. at front of integrated audiences, artists and performers ventured to speak out against the government at underground theaters and galleries. Numerous foreign-owned restaurants and nightclubs catered to a diverse clientele, including white individuals who found the status quo absurd and Black people who detested it. These individuals would also hold covert gatherings, typically at clubs that had been transformed from empty basements or someone's apartment. The gatherings themselves weren't political, but integration was by definition a political act. People would get together, socialize, and throw parties.

My mother immersed herself in that situation. She was always dancing, meeting people, and attending clubs and parties. She frequently visited the Hillbrow Tower, which at the time was among the tallest structures in Africa. On the top floor was a nightclub with a spinning dance floor. Although thrilling, it was nonetheless risky. Clubs and restaurants would occasionally close, but not always. Sometimes the artists and audience members were arrested, and other times they weren't. A roll of the dice was used. My mother was always unsure of who to trust because she was afraid someone may turn her in to the police. Reports from neighbors would be exchanged. The white men's girlfriends in my mom's apartment complex had every reason to complain about a black woman— presumably a prostitute—living with them. Additionally, you need to keep in mind that Black people were also employed by the government. My mother might have been a spy disguised as a maid or a prostitute, sent into Hillbrow to spy on white people who were breaking the law, as far as her white neighbors knew. Everyone believes that everyone else is the police, which is how a police state operates.

My mother began spending more and more time with the tall Swiss man down the corridor in 206 because she felt comfortable with him despite living alone in the city and not being able to trust anyone. He was 46 years old. Her age was twenty-four. She was wild and free; he was quiet and reserved. They would go to underground parties and dance at the nightclub with the spinning dance floor, and she would drop by his apartment to talk. Something made sense.

I am aware that my parents had a sincere relationship and love for one another. I witnessed it. I can't say, however, how romantic their connection was or how much they were merely friends. Children don't ask questions about these topics. I only know that she proposed to me one day.

She informed him, "I want to have a child."

He declared, "I don't want children."

"I didn't request that you become a parent. I begged you to assist me in getting my child. All I want from you is the sperm.

"I'm a Catholic," he declared. "We don't act in that manner."

She answered, "You do realize that I could sleep with you and leave and you wouldn't know whether you had a child or not." But that's not what I want. In order for me to live in peace, please honor me by saying "yes." I want you to give me a child so I can have one of my own. You won't have any duties, but you can view it as much as you like. You are not required to speak to it. There is no cost to you. Make this kid for me, please.

My mother found part of the attraction in the fact that this man didn't really desire a family with her and was legally barred from having one. Instead of a man taking over her life, she desired a child. I am aware that my father repeatedly said no for a considerable amount of time. In the end, he agreed. I will always be unable to answer why he said yes.

Yes, my mother checked into Hillbrow Hospital for a planned C-section delivery on February 20, 1984, which was nine months later. She was alone, estranged from her family, and pregnant by a man she was not allowed to meet in public. A half-white, half-black infant who broke numerous laws, statutes, and regulations—I was born a crime—was extracted by the physicians when they carried her up to the delivery room and cut into her belly.

There was an awkward moment when the physicians exclaimed, "Huh," after pulling me out. That baby has incredibly light skin. There was no male around to claim credit, based on a cursory glance around the delivery room.

They questioned, "Who is the father?"

My mother mentioned the small, landlocked nation in the west of South Africa, saying, "His father is from Swaziland."

They undoubtedly realized she was lying, but they needed an explanation, so they decided to believe it. Everything on your birth certificate was designated by the government under apartheid, including your race, nationality, and tribe. Everything needed to be put into categories. I was born in KaNgwane, the semi-sovereign country of the Swazi people residing in South Africa, according to my mother's false claim. Although I am Xhosa, my birth certificate does not reflect this. Furthermore, it makes no mention of my Swiss heritage, which the government would not permit. It just states that I'm a foreign national.

My birth certificate does not include my father. He has never been my father in a formal sense. And as promised, my mother was ready for him to stay out of it. When she left the hospital, she took me to her new apartment, which she had rented for herself in Joubert Park, the area next to Hillbrow. Without a baby, she visited him the following week. He asked where I was, which surprised her. She remarked, "You stated that you were not interested in getting involved." And he hadn't, but after I came into the world, he saw that he couldn't have a son living nearby and not be involved in my life. Thus, to the extent that our unique circumstances permitted, the three of us established a sort of family. My mother and I shared a home. When we had the chance, we would slip over to see my dad.

I was evidence of their criminality, when most children are evidence of their parents' love. My father and I could only spend time together indoors. He would have to cross the street from us if we left the house. I spent a lot of time at Joubert Park with my mom. It's Johannesburg's Central Park, which has lovely gardens, a zoo, and a gigantic chessboard with pieces the size of humans. My dad once attempted to accompany us while I was a toddler, according to my mother. When he was walking quite a distance away from us at the park, I screamed, "Daddy! Daddy! Daddy!" and went after him. People began to search. His panic caused him to flee. I pursued him because I believed it to be a game.

A light-skinned child with a black lady would create too many questions, therefore I was also unable to stroll with my mother. She could wrap me up and transport me wherever when I was a newborn, but that was shortly out of the question. I was a huge youngster, a gigantic baby. You would have assumed I was two when I was one. You would have assumed I was four when I was two. I could not be concealed.

 My mother discovered the flaws in the system, just as she had done with her apartment and her maids' clothes. Having two parents who were both colored was not unlawful, but being mixed—that is, having a black parent and a white parent—was. Thus, as a child of color, my mother relocated me all over the world. While she was at work, she was able to leave me in a creche in a colorful neighborhood. In our apartment complex, there was a woman of color named Queen. My mom would ask her to accompany us whenever we wanted to go to the park. Queen would pretend to be my mother while walking with me, and my mother would follow a few paces behind, pretending to be the maid employed by the woman of color. I have thousands of photos of me going for walks with this woman who isn't my mother but looks like me. Additionally, my mother is the black woman standing behind us who appears to be photobombing the photo. My mom would take the chance of walking me alone if there wasn't a woman of color to accompany us. If the cops arrived, she would have to abandon me and act as though I weren't hers, treating me like a bag of cannabis, even though she would still grasp my hand or carry me.

 The prodigal daughter returned because my mother wanted me to know her family and they to know me, even though she hadn't seen them in three years when I was born. I would spend weeks at a time, usually during the holidays, with my grandmother in Soweto, even though we lived in town. It feels like we actually lived there because I have so many memories of it.

So progressive were the architects of apartheid that they planned for Soweto to be bombed. With about a million residents, the township was a city unto itself. Only two roads led in and out. That allowed the soldiers to enclose us and put an end to any uprising. Additionally, the air force could fly over and bomb the living daylights out of everyone if the monkeys ever lost their mind and attempted to escape their cage. I was unaware as a child that my grandmother lived in the middle of a bull's-eye.

Even though it was challenging to navigate the city, we succeeded. There were so many people going to and from work—black, white, and colored—that we could get lost in the throng. But in Soweto, only Black people were allowed. Someone who looked like me was far more difficult to disguise, and the government was keeping a closer eye on things. You hardly ever saw police in the white sections, and when you did, it was Officer Friendly in his ironed pants and collared shirt. The police were an occupying force in Soweto. They wore shirts without collars. Their attire was riot gear. They had become militaristic. They were known as flying squads because they would suddenly appear atop armored personnel carriers, or hippos as we called them, which were tanks with massive tires and slotted holes in the side from which they could fire their weapons. A hippo wasn't tampered with by you. You ran when you spotted one. That was just the way things were. Insurrection was rife in the township; someone was always marching or demonstrating someplace, and it had to be put down. I would hear gunshots, cries, and tear gas being thrown into crowds while I was playing at my grandmother's house.

I was five or six years old when apartheid was finally ending, and that's when I remember the hippos and the flying squads. We could never risk the police spotting me, so I had never seen them before. My grandma wouldn't allow me go outside whenever we traveled to Soweto. "No, no, no," she said if she was observing me. He stays inside the house. I could play in the yard, behind the wall, but not in the street. The remaining youngsters and children were playing in the street there. The local kids, my cousins, would open the gate, go out and roam freely, and return at sunset. I would implore my grandma to step outside.

"Please. Could I please go play with my cousins?

"No! You will be taken by them!

She was referring to the police, but for a long time I assumed she meant that the other kids were going to steal me. Kids could be taken. The kids were abducted. If you are a child of the wrong hue in the wrong neighborhood, the government may intervene, take custody away from your parents, and send you to an orphanage. The government used its network of impipis, or anonymous snitchers who would report suspected activities, to police the townships. Additionally, there were the Blackjacks, who were black police officers. The neighbor of my grandma was a blackjack player. When she snuck me in and out of the house, she had to make sure dad wasn't looking.

My grandmother still recounts how, at the age of three, I dug a hole in the driveway beneath the gate, wriggled through, and fled because I was tired of being a prisoner. Everyone went into a panic. They sent out a search party and found me. I was putting everyone in risk, but I didn't realize it. My mom might have been sent to prison, my grandmother might have been arrested, the family might have been deported, and I would have most likely been sent to a home for colored children.

I was therefore kept indoors. The memories I have of my early years, save from those few times I went for a walk in the park, are almost exclusively of me alone at my grandmother's house or with my mother in her small apartment. There were no pals for me. Aside from my cousins, I knew no children. I was good at being by myself, so I wasn't a lonely kid. I would create imaginative worlds, play with my toy, and read books. My mind was where I resided. I continue to exist just in my mind. You may still leave me alone for hours at a time, and I'm quite content to amuse myself. I need to keep in mind to socialize.

It goes without saying that under apartheid, I was not the only kid born to black and white parents. I constantly run upon other mixed South Africans when around the world today. The beginnings of our stories are the same. Our ages are around the same. In Hillbrow or Cape Town, their parents met at an underground party. Their apartment was illegal. The distinction is that they departed in almost every other instance. Being a mixed family under apartheid was simply intolerable, so the white parents snuck them out through Lesotho or Botswana and raised them in exile in England, Germany, or Switzerland.

Mandela's election allowed us to live in freedom at last. The exiles began to come home. Around the age of seventeen, I had my first encounter. When he shared his story with me, I thought, "Wait, what? You mean we had the option to go? Was that a possibility? Consider being flung from an aircraft. You break all of your bones when you hit the ground, go to the hospital to recover, move on, and eventually put the incident behind you. Then one day, someone informs you about parachutes. I felt like way. Why we had stayed was beyond me. I asked my mother as soon as I got home.

"Why? Why didn't we simply go? What prevented us from visiting Switzerland?

As obstinate as ever, she uttered, "Because I am not Swiss." "This is my nation. Why should I go?

Chapter 3: Trevor, Pray

My grandfather, who was the father of my mother, was the sole semi-regular male figure in my existence. He was a formidable individual. Although he was divorced from my grandmother and did not reside with us, he was present. Temperance Noah was his name, which was peculiar given that he was not at all a man of moderation. Loud and raucous, he was. In the community, he was known as "Tat Shisha," which is a loose translation of "the smokin' hot grandpa." And that is precisely his identity. He harbored affection for the women, and they harbored affection for him. On random afternoons, he would don his finest suit and leisurely meander through the streets of Soweto, captivating all the women he encountered and eliciting laughter from all. He possessed a large, dazzling smile that was accompanied by brilliant white teeth that were actually false. He would remove them at home, and I would observe him perform the act of eating his own visage.

We were unaware of his bipolar disorder until much later in life; prior to that, we considered him eccentric. At least once, he borrowed my mother's vehicle to purchase bread and milk from the store. He vanished and did not return home until late that evening, when we were well past the point of needing the milk or the bread. It was discovered that he had passed a young woman at the bus stop. He offered her a transport to her residence, which was three hours away, as he believed that no beautiful woman should be forced to wait for a bus. My mother was incensed with him because he had squandered an entire cylinder of gasoline, which would have sufficed to transport us to work and school for two weeks.

He was uncontrollable when he was awake, but his mood fluctuations were erratic. He had been a boxer in his youth, and one day he claimed that I had disrespected him, and as a result, he wanted to box me. He was in his eighties. I was twelve years old. He was encircling me with his fists raised. "Let's depart, Trevah!" Please! Raise your hands! Please strike me! I will demonstrate that I am still a man. We should depart! I was unable to strike him because I was unwilling to inflict harm on my elder. Additionally, I had never been involved in a physical altercation, and I was determined that my initial altercation would not be with an eighty-year-old man. I immediately rushed to my mother, who successfully convinced him to cease. He remained seated in his chair for the entirety of the day following his pugilistic fury, failing to speak or move.

My mom was often worried about becoming poisoned, so we didn't spend much time with Temperance's second family in the Meadowlands. This was an inevitable event. Since the first family was the heirs, there was always a possibility that the second family would poison them. With impoverished people, it was similar to Game of Thrones. My mother would warn me before we entered that house.

"Don't eat the food, Trevor."

"But I'm going hungry."

"No. They could contaminate us.

"All right, so why don't I simply ask Jesus to remove the poison from the food?"

"Hey Trevor! "Sun'qhela!"

As a result, I only occasionally saw my grandfather, and once he passed away, women took over the house.

My mom was joined by my aunt Sibongile, who had two children, my cousins Mlungisi and Bulelwa, with her first husband, Dinky. Sibongile was the mother hen, a powerful woman with a large chest and all-around strength. As his name suggests, Dinky was just that—dinky. He was a little man. He wasn't actually abusive. It seemed more like he made an effort to be abusive but struggled with it. He was making an effort to live up to his idea of what a husband ought to be—dominant and controlling. As a child, I recall hearing the statement, "You don't love your woman if you don't hit her." You might hear folks talking like that at pubs and on the street.

Dinky attempted to pass for this patriarch, but he wasn't. He would repeatedly punch and slap my aunt, but she would ultimately lose it and slap him down, putting him back in his proper place. "I control my woman," Dinky would say as he walked around. "Dinky, first of all, you don't," is what you would want to say. Secondly, you are not required to. since she adores you. I recall that my aunt had had enough one day. Dinky ran screaming bloody murder out of the house while I was in the yard. He was immediately followed by Sibongile, who was brandishing a pot of hot water and threatening to splash him with it. In Soweto, it was common to hear about males being sprayed with boiling water, which was frequently a woman's only option. And if it was water, guys were lucky. Hot cooking oil was utilized by some women. If the lady wished to discipline her guy, she used water. Oil indicated her want to stop it.

The matriarch of the family was my grandmother, Frances Noah. She took care of the children, cooked, cleaned, and maintained the household. Despite being slumped over from years of working in the factory, she is just five feet tall, rock hard, and still very much alive and active today. My grandmother had a bright mind and was calm and calculating, in contrast to my grandfather's large and noisy demeanor. She can tell you the day, the location, and the reason behind any event in the family history, which dates back to the 1930s. She recalls everything.

We also had my great-grandmother living with us. We gave her the name Koko. She was stooping, weak, blind, and very old—well into her nineties. Cataracts had coated her eyes, turning them white. Without someone to support her, she was unable to walk. She would sit with blankets over her shoulders, wrapped in long skirts and head scarves, next to the coal stove in the kitchen. The coal stove never shut off. It was used for bath water heating, cooking, and housing heating. Since it was the hottest place in the house, we placed her there. She would be roused in the morning and sent to the kitchen to sit. She would be taken to bed by someone at night. She spent the entire day doing it. Take a seat beside the stove. She was amazing and totally into it. She simply was unable to see and remained still.

When I was five years old, I didn't consider Koko to be a real person, even though she and my grandmother would sit and have lengthy chats. She was like a brain with a mouth because her body was immobile. Our communication was limited to command prompts and responses, like to conversing with a machine.

"Koko, good morning."

"Good morning, Trevor."

"Did you eat, Koko?"

"Yes, Trevor."

"I'm leaving, Koko."

"All right, watch out."

"Goodbye, Koko."

"Goodbye, Trevor."

It was no coincidence that I was raised in a world dominated by women. Because my father was white, apartheid prevented me from seeing him, but for nearly every child I knew on my grandmother's block in Soweto, apartheid had also taken away their fathers, albeit for different reasons. Only during the holidays were their fathers allowed to return home from their jobs working in mines. Both of their fathers had been imprisoned. Their fathers were fighting for the cause while living in exile. The community was held together by women. They would rally around the shout, "Wathint'Abafazi Wathint'imbokodo!" during the liberation war. "You hit a rock when you hit a woman." Although women were supposed to submit and obey in the home, our country acknowledged their strength.

Religion filled the void left by the absence of males in Soweto. I used to inquire about my mother's difficulty in raising me alone in the absence of a spouse. She would respond, "The mere fact that I am currently without a spouse does not imply that I have never been married." "God is my husband." Life revolved around faith for my mother, my aunt, my grandmother, and all the other women on our street. The residences on the block would be rotated for prayer meetings on a daily basis. Women and children comprised these categories exclusively. My mother would consistently request that my uncle Velile participate in the organization. He would respond, "I would participate if there were additional male members; however, I am unable to serve as the sole individual present." Subsequently, the chanting and prayer would commence, and this served

28

as his signal to depart.

We would congregate in the cramped living area of the host family's residence for these prayer meetings and establish a circle. Subsequently, we would circumambulate the circle, offering petitions. The grandmothers would engage in conversation regarding their personal affairs. "I am delighted to be present." I had a productive week at work. I received a promotion and desired to express my gratitude and praise to Jesus. Occasionally, they would retrieve their Bible and state, "This passage resonated with me; perhaps it will be beneficial to you." At that point, there would be a brief musical interlude. A leather device known as "the beat" was attached to one's palm, resembling a percussion instrument. "Masango vulekani singene eJerusalema. Masango vulekani singene eJerusalema." While everyone sang, someone would applaud in time.

That would be the course of action. Sing, pray, and pray. Sing, pray, and sing. Sing, sing, sing. Pray, pray, pray. Occasionally, it would extend for hours, concluding with a "amen." They were able to sustain that "amen" for a minimum of five minutes. " Ah-men. Ah-ah-ah-men. Ah-ah-ah-ah-men.
Ahhhhhhhhahhhhh-hhhhhh-hahhhhhhhahhhhhhahhhhhhhhhhhmen.
Men, men, men. Men, men, men.
Ahhhhh-hhhhh-hhhhh-hhhhh-hhhhh-hhhhh-hhhhh-hhhhh-hhhhmmmm
mmmennnnn-nnnnn-nnnnn-nnnnn-nnnnn-nnnnn-nnnnn-nnnnn-nnnnn-n
nnnn-nnnnn-nnnnn-nnnnn-nnnnn-nnnnn-nnnnn-nnnnn-nnnnn-nnnnn-nn
nnn-nnnnn-nnnnn-nnnnn-nnnnn-nnnnn-nnnnn-nnnnn-n." Afterward, everyone would bid each other farewell and return to their respective residences. The following evening, the same event occurred in a different residence.

I was always eager to attend the prayer meeting at my grandmother's house on Tuesday evenings for two reasons. One, I was permitted to applaud in time with the singing. And second, I enjoyed praying. My grandmother consistently expressed her appreciation for my petitions. She was of the opinion that my petitions were more potent because I prayed in English. Jesus, who is Caucasian, is universally recognized as speaking English. The Bible is written in the English language. Certainly, the Bible was not composed in English; however, it was brought to South Africa in English, and as a result, it is considered to be in English. This rendered my petitions the most effective, as prayers in English are addressed first. What is the source of this information? Observe individuals of white skin. It is evident that they are successfully communicating with the appropriate individual. Additionally, Matthew 19:14 should be considered. "Allow little children to come to me," Jesus said, "for theirs is the kingdom of heaven." Therefore, what happens when an infant prays in English? To whom does White Jesus refer? That is an extremely potent combination. "That prayer will be answered," my grandmother would say whenever I prayed. The sensation is palpable.

Something enchanting is present in Soweto. While it was true that our oppressors designed the prison, it also provided us with a sense of self-determination and control. Soweto was ours. There was an aspirational quality to it that is not present in any other context. In the United States, the aspiration is to escape the barrio. The aspiration in Soweto was to transform the ghetto, as it was impossible to exit the ghetto.

Spaza establishments and shebeens were the most prevalent. The spaza shops were informal grocery retailers. Individuals would construct a kiosk in their garage, purchase wholesale bread and eggs, and subsequently resell them in small quantities. Everyone in the township purchased items in small quantities due to the fact that no one had any money. You were unable to purchase a dozen eggs at a time, but you could get by with two, as that was all you required that morning. A quarter loaf of bread and one cup of sugar are available for purchase. The shebeens were illegal establishments located at the rear of an individual's residence. They would install an awning, place chairs in their backyard, and operate a speakeasy. The shebeens were the destination for men to consume alcohol after work, during prayer meetings, and at basically any other time of day.

People constructed dwellings in the same manner as they purchased eggs: incrementally. The government allocated a plot of land to each family in the township. Initially, you would construct a shanty on your property, which is a temporary structure composed of corrugated iron and plywood. Over time, you would accumulate funds and construct a brick fortification. A single wall. Then, you would accumulate funds and construct an additional fortification. Then, years later, a third partition and, eventually, a fourth. You now had a single room in which all members of your family could sleep, dine, and perform any other activities. Then, you would accumulate funds to purchase a roof. Afterward, windows. The object would be plastered. Then, your daughter would establish a family. Without any alternative residence, they would relocate to your residence. You would augment your brick room with an additional corrugated-iron structure and gradually transform it into a suitable space for them over the course of several years. Currently, your residence consisted of two chambers. Then, three. Potentially four. Over the course of generations, you would continue to strive to achieve the status of owning a residence.

Orlando East was the residence of my grandmother. She resided in a two-room household. The space consisted of a bedroom and a living room/kitchen/everything-else type of chamber. Some may argue that we lived in a manner that was indicative of poverty. I prefer the term "open plan." During school holidays, my mother and I would reside there. Whenever she was not with Dinky, my aunt and cousins would be present. We all slept on the floor in a single room, including my mother and me, my aunt and cousins, my uncle, my grandmother, and my great-grandmother. The adults each had their own foam mattress, and there was a large one that we would roll out into the center, and the children would sleep on it.

My grandmother rented out two shanties in the backyard to seasonal laborers and migrants. On one side of the house, there was a small peach tree in a small plot, and on the other side, my grandmother had a driveway. I never comprehended the rationale behind my grandmother's driveway. She did not possess a vehicle. She was unfamiliar with the operation of a vehicle. Nevertheless, she possessed a driveway. All of our neighbors had driveways, some of which were adorned with elaborate, cast-iron gates. Additionally, none of them owned automobiles. It was impossible for the majority of these families to acquire automobiles in the future. Despite the fact that there was a mere one vehicle per thousand individuals, nearly every household had a driveway. It was almost as though the construction of the driveway was a form of commanding the vehicle to occur. The narrative of Soweto is the narrative of the driveways. It is a location that inspires optimism.

Regrettably, there was one aspect of your residence that you could never enhance, regardless of how extravagantly decorated it was: your commode. There was no interior running water; instead, there was a communal outdoor tap and an outdoor toilet that were shared by six or seven houses. The lavatory was located in a corrugated-iron outhouse that was shared by the neighboring residences. On the inside, there was a concrete slab with a hole and a plastic toilet seat atop it. A lid had been present at one time, but it had been shattered and vanished a long time ago. We were unable to purchase toilet paper, so a wire hanger with old newspaper was affixed to the wall adjacent to the seat for you to cleanse. Although the newspaper was cumbersome, I was able to remain informed while conducting my business.

My grandmother, who was approximately five years old at the time, left me at home for a few hours to run errands. I was reading while lying on the floor of the bedroom. I was compelled to leave, but the rain was relentless. I was apprehensive about venturing outside to use the restroom, as I anticipated being drenched as I ran, the water dripping from the leaky ceiling, the damp newspaper, and the flies attacking me from below. Afterward, I developed a notion. What is the purpose of the outhouse? Why not place some newspaper on the floor and conduct myself in a manner reminiscent of a puppy? That appeared to be an extraordinary concept. So that is what I did. I removed the newspaper, placed it on the kitchen floor, undid my trousers, and squatted to retrieve it.

When you're taking a dump, you're never more yourself. There comes a time when you recognize yourself. I am this person. You can urinate without thinking twice, but poo requires more thought. Have you ever stared into a baby's shit-filled eyes? It's experiencing a flash of acute self-awareness. That's ruined for you by the outhouse. No one should be denied their time, yet you are deprived of it because of the rain and the insects. I thought, "Wow," as I squatted and poop on the kitchen floor that day. No flies are present. No stress exists. This is fantastic. I'm having a great time. I was rather proud of myself for making the decision, and I knew I had made a great one. I had arrived at the point where I could unwind and spend time alone. Then, while I was idly scanning the room, I looked to my left and saw Koko standing a few feet away, next to the coal burner.

It was similar to the scene in Jurassic Park where the T. rex is right there when the kids turn around. Her eyes darted around the room, wide open and clouded white. Her nose was beginning to wrinkle, and even though I knew she couldn't see me, she could tell something wasn't right.

I went into a panic. I was in the middle. When you're in the middle, all you can do is finish crap. I chose to finish as softly and slowly as possible because that was my only choice. Then: the newspaper with the softest splat of a young boy's poop. Koko's head jerked in the direction of the noise.

"Who's there? Hello? Hello?

I went cold. I waited while holding my breath.

"Who's there? Hello?

I remained silent, waited, and then resumed.

"Is there anyone there? Is that you, Trevor? Frances? Hello? Hello?

She began yelling at the entire family. "Nombuyiselo? Sibongile? Mlungisi? Bulelwa? Who is present? What is going on?

It felt like a game, with a blind woman using sonar to try to find me while I was trying to conceal. I froze each time she yelled out. There would be no sound at all. "Hello! Who's there? I would stop and wait for her to return to her seat before continuing.

After what seemed like an eternity, I finally finished. I got up, picked up the newspaper—which isn't the quietest thing—and folded it over slowly. It was crinkly. "Who is present?" I stopped and waited once more. After that, I folded it over once more, went to the trash can, put my sin in the bottom, and carefully covered it with the remaining trash. Subsequently, I crouched on the floor mattress in the opposite room and feigned sleep. Koko didn't know that the poo was done, and there was no outhouse involved.

The mission has been completed.

The rain ended an hour later. My grandma returned home. Koko shouted out to her as soon as she entered.

"Frances! I'm glad you're here. Something is in the house.

"What was it?"

"I don't know, but there was a smell and I could hear it."

My grandmother began to sniff the air. "Oh Lord! Yes, I can also smell it. Is that a rat? Was there a death? Without a doubt, it is in the house.

They debated it back and forth, both of them extremely worried, and then my mother arrived home from work because it was getting late. My grandmother yelled out to her as soon as she entered.

"Oh, Nombuyiselo! Nombuyiselo! Something is in the home!

"What? What are you saying?

Koko described the narrative, the noises, and the scents to her.

Then my mother, who has an excellent sense of smell, began sniffing around the kitchen. I can smell it, yes. I can locate it. I can locate it. She proceeded to the trash can. "It's inside." She removed the trash, took out the folded newspaper underneath, and when she opened it, my tiny turd was within. Gran was shown it by her.

"Observe!"

"What? What brought it there?

Still blind and confined to her chair, Koko was desperate to learn what was going on.

"What's happening?" she exclaimed. "What's happening? Have you located it?

Mom said, "It's shit." "The dustbin's bottom contains shit."

"How? "Koko said." "No one was present!"

"Are you certain that nobody was present?"

Indeed. I yelled at everyone. No one showed up.

My mom let out a gasp. We've been enchanted! It's a devil!

This was the obvious conclusion for my mother. Because witchcraft operates in this manner. In the event that you or your house have been cursed, there is always evidence of the demon's existence, such as a talisman or totem, a tuft of hair, or a cat's head.

After my mother discovered the turd, chaos ensued. This was a severe matter. They had proof. She entered the bedroom.

"Trevor! Trevor! Get up!

"What?" Playing dumb, I said. "What's happening?!"

"Come on! A demon is there in the house!

She grabbed my hand and pulled me from the bed. It was time for action, and everyone was on deck. We had to walk outside and burn the feces as our first action. That's what you do with witchcraft; burning the actual object is the only way to eradicate it. My mom lit a match, placed the newspaper containing my small poo on the driveway, and set it on fire after we went outside to the yard. After that, my grandmother and mother stood around the blazing mess, singing praise songs and praying.

When a demon is present, the entire town must band together to expel it, thus the chaos didn't end there. The demon may leave our home and visit yours, where he will curse you if you do not participate in the prayer. We therefore required everyone. Someone sounded the alarm. The call was placed. My small elderly grandmother was outside the gate, phoning the other elderly grandmothers for an urgent prayer meeting while she went up and down the street. "Come on! We've been enchanted!

I was at a loss for what to do as I stood there with my feces blazing in the driveway and my elderly grandmother frantically walking up and down the block. I couldn't come clean, even though I knew there wasn't a demon. The concealing I'd have to go through? Thank God. When it came to a hiding, being honest was never the best course of action. I said nothing.

Shortly after, at least a dozen grannies poured through the gate and up

34

the driveway, carrying their Bibles. They all went inside. The house was full. This was by far the largest prayer meeting we had ever held—the largest event in our home's history, in general. In the circle, everyone sat and prayed, and the prayers were powerful. Speaking in tongues, the grandmothers were swaying back and forth, chanting, and mumbling. I was trying my hardest to keep my head down and avoid becoming involved. My grandma then grabbed me from behind, dragged me to the center of the circle, and met my eyes.

"Pray, Trevor."

"Yes!" answered my mom. "Aid us! Trevor, please pray. Ask God to exterminate the demon!

I was afraid. I thought that prayer had great power. I knew my prayers had been answered. Therefore, God would murder me if I prayed for him to kill the thing that left the shit and that thing turned out to be me. I went cold. I was at a loss for what to do. However, I prayed, bumbling through as best I could, because all the grandmothers were staring at me and waiting for me to do so.

"Dear Lord, please protect us from whoever did this, but... we don't know exactly what happened and maybe it was a big misunderstanding, so maybe we shouldn't be quick to judge when we don't know the whole story. Of course, Heavenly Father, you know best, but maybe this time it wasn't actually a demon because who can tell for sure, so maybe cut whoever it was a break."

I didn't give my best effort. I finally wrapped it up and took a seat again. The prayers went on. It continued for a while. Sing, pray, pray. Sing, pray, sing. Sing, sing, sing. Continue to pray. After the huge "amen," everyone said good night and left for their homes, and everyone at last felt that the demon had gone and life could go on.

I felt awful that night. I silently prayed, "God, I am so sorry for all of this," before going to bed. I am aware that this was not cool. Because I was aware that God hears your petitions. Your father is God. He is the one who looks for you and is always there for you. I had put Him through two hours of old grannies praying when I knew that, with all the agony and suffering in the world, He had more important things to deal with than my trash. When you pray, He stops, takes His time, and listens.

Chapter 4: Chameleon

I was playing with my cousins one afternoon. They were my patients, and I was a physician. I unintentionally punctured my cousin Bulelwa's eardrum while using a pair of matches to operate on her ear. Hell erupted. From the kitchen, my grandmother rushed in. "Kwenzeka ntoni?" "What is going on?!" Blood was oozing from my cousin's skull. We were all in tears. Bulelwa's ear was bandaged by my grandma, who took care to halt the bleeding. However, we continued to cry. Because it was obvious that we had done something improper, and we were aware that we would face consequences. After finishing with Bulelwa's ear, my grandmother pulled out a belt and gave her a severe beating. Then she also gave Mlungisi a severe beating. I wasn't touched by her.

My mother returned home from work later that evening. She discovered my grandmother sobbing at the kitchen table and my cousin with a bandage over her ear.

"What's happening?" my mother asked.

"Oh," she continued, "Nombuyiselo." "Trevor is really mischievous. He is the most mischievous child I have ever encountered in my life.

"Then you ought to strike him."

"I can't strike him."

"Why not?"

She explained, "Because I don't know how to hit a white child." "A child of color, I get it. If you strike a black child, they will continue to be black. When you strike him, Trevor, he becomes red, yellow, green, and blue. Those are colors I have never seen before. I'm afraid I'll shatter him. I have no desire to murder a white person. I'm terrified. I will not come in contact with him. She also never did.

I was treated like a white person by my grandmother. The only difference is that my grandfather was considerably more extreme. He referred to me as "Mastah." As though he were my chauffeur, he insisted on driving me in the automobile. "Mastah has to take the back seat at all times." I never questioned him about it. What could I have said? "Grandfather, I think your understanding of race is faulty." No. I was five years old. I took a seat toward the rear.

I can't even begin to list all the benefits of being "white" in a black family. I was enjoying myself immensely. I was treated more leniently than the black children, which is essentially what the American legal system does. I received a warning and got away with misbehaving, something my relatives would have been punished for. In addition, I was far more mischievous than either of my cousins. It was far from it. I was the one who would take Granny's cookies if something broke. I was problematic.

The one power I really dreaded was my mother. She felt that you pamper the child if you spare the rod. However, everyone else dismissed me, saying, "No, he's different." My upbringing taught me how simple it is for white people to become accustomed to a system that gives them all the benefits. I was aware that my cousins were being beaten for actions I had taken, but I had no interest in altering my grandmother's viewpoint because doing so would result in my own beating. Why would I do that? In order for me to feel better? I didn't feel any better after being beaten. I had an option. I could eat my grandmother's cookies or advocate for racial justice in our household. I choose the cookies.

The population of Soweto was close to one million. They were ninety-nine percent black, and then there was me. Just because of the hue of my skin, I was well-known in my area. People used me as a signpost when giving directions since I was so distinctive. "The Makhalima Street residence." There's a boy with light skin in the corner. There, make a right.

The children on the street would shout, "Indoda yomlungu!" whenever they spotted me. "The man with white skin!" A few of them would flee. Some would beckon their parents to come take a look. To check if I was real, people would rush up to touch me. Chaos reigned. At the time, I didn't realize that the other children actually didn't know what a white person was. The township's black children stayed there. Not many folks owned televisions. They had witnessed the white police arrive, but they had never had a face-to-face encounter with a white person.

When I would walk in during a funeral, the people who had lost a loved one would look up and see me, and their tears would cease. They would begin to whisper. Then they would wave and exclaim, "Oh!" as if they were more surprised that I had entered than that their loved ones had passed away. Because a white individual attended the funeral, I believe that people thought that the deceased was more significant.

In my mind, white, black, and brown were like different kinds of chocolate, even though I knew as a child that people were colored differently. Mom represented the dark chocolate, Dad the white chocolate, and me the milk chocolate. We were all chocolate, though. I was unaware that any of it was related to "race." I was ignorant of the concept of race. My mother never called me mixed or my father white. I therefore assumed that the other children in Soweto had misidentified my hue, as if they hadn't learned it correctly, when they referred to me as "white" despite the fact that I was light brown. "Yes, my friend," I said. You have mistaken aqua with turquoise. I understand how you made that error. You are not unique.

I quickly discovered that language was the most effective means of bridging the racial divide. Families from various tribes and countries lived in Soweto, which was a melting pot. Since I grew up in a household where learning languages was the only choice, I acquired multiple languages, even though the majority of children in the township only spoke their native tongue. English was the first language I spoke because of my mother. Speaking English is the one thing that can offer you an advantage if you're Black in South Africa. The language of money is English. Intelligence is connected with the ability to comprehend English. English proficiency might make the difference between landing a job and being unemployed. If you're in the dock, your English could mean the difference between a fine and jail time.

When I lived with my mother, I witnessed how she handled issues, crossed boundaries, and navigated the world using language. Once, while we were at a store, the owner turned to face his security guy and yelled, "Volg daai swartes, netnou steel hulle iets," in Afrikaans. "If those black people steal something, follow them."

My mother turned around and exclaimed, "Hoekom volg jy nie daai swartes sodat jy hulle kan help kry waarna hulle soek nie?" in lovely, fluent Afrikaans. "Why don't you help these Black people find what they're looking for by following them?"

"Ag, jammer!" he said in Afrikaans, expressing regret. The ironic part is that he only apologized for directing his hatred towards us, not for being racist in the first place. He said, "Oh, I'm so sorry." "I assumed you were just like the other black people. You are aware of their fondness for stealing.

I picked up my mother's language skills. I would simulcast, or deliver the show in your native tongue. People simply strolling along the street would give me weird looks. They'd inquire, "Where are you from?" I would respond with the same accent and in the language they had used to address me. A moment of bewilderment would pass, and then the suspicious expression would vanish. "Oh, all right. You seemed like a stranger to me. We're good then."

It became a tool that benefited me my whole life. One day as a young man I was strolling down the street, and a group of Zulu males was walking behind me, closing in on me, and I could hear them chatting to one another about how they were going to mug me. "Le autie yomlungu asibambe." Ngemuva kwakhe phuma ngapha mina ngizoqhamuka. "We should get this white man. I'll follow him as you go to his left. I was at a loss for what to do. Because I was unable to flee, I simply spun around and exclaimed, "Kodwa bafwethu yingani singavele sibambe umuntu inkunzi? Asenzeni. Mina ngikulindele. "Hey everyone, how about we all mug someone together? I'm prepared. Let's get it done.

After a brief period of shock, they burst out laughing. I'm sorry, man. We mistook you for someone else. We had no intention of stealing anything from you. We were attempting to rob white individuals. Enjoy your day, dude. They were ready to do me serious harm, until they felt we were part of the same tribe, and then we were cool. That, and so many more little occurrences in my life, made me realize that language, even more than color, determines who you are to people.

I became a chameleon. Although my color remained the same, I could alter how you saw it. I would respond to you in Zulu if you spoke to me in that language. I would respond to you in Tswana if you spoke to me in that language. Even if I might not have looked like you, I was you if I spoke like you.

South Africa's prestigious private schools began to accept students of all races when apartheid was ending. Through her company, which provided scholarships and bursaries to disadvantaged families, my mother was able to secure me admission to Maryvale College, a pricey private Catholic institution. Nuns teach the classes. Friday Mass. the entirety of it. When I was three, I began preschool there, and when I was five, I started primary school.

There were a variety of children in my class. Children of color, Indian children, white children, and black children. The majority of the white children were fairly prosperous. Almost all children of color weren't. However, we were all seated at the same table due to scholarships. We wore the identical gray skirts, gray trousers, and maroon jackets. Our books were identical. Our teachers were the same. Racial segregation did not exist. Each clique has a mix of races.

Though it was more commonplace, children were nevertheless mocked and bullied for being overweight or skinny, tall or short, intelligent or stupid. I don't recall any instances of racial taunting. I didn't learn to set boundaries for what I should and shouldn't like. I was free to explore on my own. I was attracted to white girls. I was attracted to black girls. I was not asked what I was. My name was Trevor.

Although it was a fantastic experience, I was shielded from reality as a result. Maryvale was a haven that protected me from reality and allowed me to avoid having to make a difficult choice. However, the actual world remains. There is racism. Just because it doesn't happen to you doesn't mean that it doesn't happen to other people. And you have to make a decision eventually. either white or black. Choose a side. You can attempt to avoid it. Life will eventually compel you to choose a side, even if you claim that you don't.

I transferred from Maryvale to the government-run H. A. Jack Primary at the conclusion of grade six. Before I started, I had to take an aptitude test, and the school counselor informed me that I would be in the "A" or "smart" classes based on the test results. On the first day of school, I arrived at my classroom. Nearly every one of the thirty or so children in my class was white. There was me, one Indian child, and possibly one or two black children.

Then it was recess. Black children were everywhere on the playground when we were there. As if someone had opened a tap and all the darkness had poured out, it was an ocean of black. Where were they all hiding, I thought? I was left standing in the center, completely bewildered, while the white students I had met that morning went in one direction and the black kids went in another. Were we to get together later? I couldn't comprehend what was going on.

At the age of eleven, I felt as though I was seeing my nation for the first time. There is no segregation in the townships since everyone is black. We were the only Black people in the white world whenever my mother took me to a white church, and she never distanced herself from anyone. She was indifferent. She would immediately approach and take a seat with the white folks. Additionally, the children at Maryvale were interacting and hanging out together. Prior to that day, I had never witnessed individuals occupying the same area but choosing to have no relationship with one another. I could see and feel the boundaries being drawn in an instant. Groups walked down the hall, up the stairs, and across the yard in patterns of color. It was crazy. I turned to face the white children I had met earlier in the day. I had assumed that they were the majority at the school ten minutes prior. In comparison to everyone else, I now noticed how few of them there were.

I stood clumsily by myself in the center of the playground, in this no-man's land. Fortunately, Theesan Pillay, an Indian student in my class, came to my aid. Theesan had immediately recognized me as another blatant outsider because he was one of the few Indian students in the school. He hurried over to say hello. "Hi there, fellow outlier! I have you in my class. Who are you? What is your story? We struck up a conversation and clicked. To my confused Oliver, he took me under his wing and called me the Artful Dodger.

The fact that I could speak multiple African languages came up during our chat, and Theesan thought that the most amazing trick was a colored child speaking black languages. He led me to a group of African American children. He said to them, "He'll show you he understands you if you say something." I responded to a child in Zulu after he stated something in that language. Everyone applauded. I responded to another child in Xhosa when he said something in that language. Everyone applauded. Theesan took me to see various black children on the playground for the remainder of recess. "Prove your trick to them. Take care of your language skills.

The Black children were captivated. During the apartheid era, white people were constantly indoctrinated that African languages were inferior to their own, hence it was uncommon to find a white or colored person speaking an African language in South Africa. Therefore, the black children liked me right away since I could speak African languages.

They questioned, "Why do you speak our languages?"

I said, "Because I'm Black, just like you."

"You're not Black."

"Yes, I am."

"No, you're not. Did you fail to perceive yourself?

At first, they were perplexed. They believed that I was a colored person because of my hue, but the fact that we spoke the same languages indicated that I was a member of their tribe. They simply needed some time to figure it out. I also took a moment.

I asked one of them, "Hey, why don't I see you guys in any of my classes?" at one point. They were in the B courses, which were also the black classes, as it turned out. I returned to the A classes that same afternoon, but by the end of the day, I had come to the conclusion that they weren't for me. All of a sudden, I recognized my tribe and desired to be among them. The school counselor was the person I visited.

I said to her, "I want to switch over." "I want to attend the B classes."

She didn't understand. "Oh, no," she said. "I doubt that's what you want to do."

"Why not?"

"Because those children are,"

"No, I'm not sure. What are you saying?

"Look," she remarked, "you're a bright youngster. You wish to avoid that class.

However, aren't the classes identical? English is English. Math is math.

Yes, but those kids in that class are going to keep you back. You wish to be a member of the intelligent class.

"However, the B class must contain some intelligent students."

"No, there aren't."

"But there are all of my friends."

"Those kids are not people you want to be friends with."

"Yes, I do."

We walked back and forth. At last, she issued a severe warning to me.

"Are you aware of how this will affect your future? Are you aware of what you're giving up? Your options for the remainder of your life will be impacted by this.

"I'll take that risk."

I joined the black students in the B classes. I made the decision that I would rather be held back with individuals I liked than advance with strangers.

Being at H. A. I became aware that I was Black thanks to Jack. I had never had to make a decision before that recess, but when I did, I went with black. I didn't live my life staring at myself, even though the world perceived me as colored. I've been observing other people my entire life. The folks around me were Black, and I identified with them. My mother, grandmother, and cousins are all Black. I was raised as a Black person. I got along with the white kids because I had a white father and had attended a white Sunday school, but I didn't belong with them. I did not belong to their tribe. But I was greeted by the black children. Join them, they said. "You're playing along with us." I didn't attempt to be the black kid all the time. I just was among the black kids.

Chapter 5: The Second Girl

"I chose to have you because I wanted something to love and something that would love me unconditionally in return," my mother used to say to me. I was the result of her quest for acceptance. Nowhere did she ever feel like she belonged. She was not her father's property, her mother's property, or her siblings' property. She desired something of her own because she had nothing growing up.

Being a tomboy, feisty, and disobedient, my mother was the troublemaker. My grandmother didn't know how to bring her up. The ongoing conflict between them wiped out any love they may have had. However, my mother loved her father, Temperance, who was a charming and dynamic man. She joined him on his frantic trips, gallivanting with him. When he went out to drink with the shebeens, she would accompany him. She only wanted to be with him and please him. Her desire to be with him was only heightened by the fact that she was constantly swatted away by his girlfriends, who didn't appreciate having a reminder of his past marriage around.

My mother informed my grandmother that she no longer wanted to live with her when she was nine years old. Her desire was to live with her dad. Gran responded, "Go if that's what you want." My mom joyfully jumped into Temperance's car when he arrived to pick her up, eager to spend time with the man she loved. He didn't want her either, so he sent her to live with his sister in the Xhosa country of Transkei instead of taking her to live with him in the Meadowlands, without even explaining why. The middle child was my mom. The firstborn and oldest was her sister. The only son and heir to the family name was her brother. Both of them remained in Soweto, where their parents reared and looked after them. However, my mother was not wanted. The second girl was her. China is the only place where she would be less valuable.

It was twelve years before my mother saw her family again. Fourteen relatives, fourteen children from fourteen different moms and fathers, shared a hut with her. The children that were unwanted or that no one could afford to support had been sent back to the country to live on this aunt's farm, while all of the husbands and uncles had left for the metropolis in search of employment.

In contrast to the beautiful, irrigated, and verdant white countryside of South Africa, the black areas were overpopulated, overgrazed, and their soil was deteriorating. Families hardly made ends meet beyond subsistence farming, except from the pitiful income sent home from the city. She had not been adopted by my mother's aunt out of altruism. Her purpose was to labor. My mother used to say, "I was one of the oxen, one of the cows." Before the heat baked the dirt as hard as cement and made it too hot to be anywhere but in the shade, she and her cousins were up at half past four, plow fields, and herd animals.

One chicken may be enough to serve fourteen kids for dinner. To receive a handful of meat, a sip of gravy, or even a bone to extract some marrow from, my mom would have to battle with the older children. And that was the only time there was any dinner meal. She would grab food from the pigs when there wasn't. She would rob the dogs of their food. She would leap for the crumbs that the farmers would put out for the animals. Let the animals fend for themselves; she was hungry. She would practically eat dirt at times. To make a grayish milk, she would go down to the river, gather clay from the bank, and combine it with water. To feel full, she would drink that.

However, despite the government's Bantu education policies, my mother was fortunate that a mission school had managed to remain open in her village. She received English instruction from a white pastor there. Despite without food, shoes, and even a pair of underpants, she was able to communicate in English. She was literate. She quit working on the farm when she was old enough and found employment in a nearby town's factory. She made school uniforms using a sewing machine. At the conclusion of each day, she received a dish of food as payment. Since she had earned it on her own, she used to claim that it was the greatest food she had ever had. She owed no one anything and was not a burden to anyone.

My mom's aunt became unwell when she became twenty-one, and the family was unable to support her in Transkei. In a letter to my grandmother, my mother requested that she pay the about thirty rand cost of a train ticket so that she may return home. My mother took the secretarial course back in Soweto, which helped her get a foothold in the white-collar industry. She kept working, but since she was living under my grandmother's roof, she was not permitted to keep her earnings. My grandmother required that all of the money that my mom brought home from her job as a secretary go to the family. My mother was now responsible for providing the family with a refrigerator, an oven, and a radio.

Black families tend to spend all of their time attempting to resolve the issues from the past. That's the curse of being poor and Black, and it's a curse that is passed down through the generations. My mom refers to it as "the black tax." Instead of being able to use your education and abilities to advance, you lose everything attempting to bring everyone behind you back to zero since the generations that came before you have been pillaged. My mom fled because she was working for the family in Soweto and had no more freedom than she had in Transkei. Determined to sleep in public restrooms and depend on the generosity of prostitutes until she could fend for herself, she sprinted all the way down to the train station, hopped on a train, and vanished into the city.

None of the things my mother told me were ever motivated by self-pity, but rather to make sure I would never take for granted how we ended up where we were. She would advise, "Learn from your past and be better because of it, but don't cry about it." Pain is a part of life. Don't hang on to the hurt; instead, let it sharpen you. Don't harbor resentment. Furthermore, she was never. She never voiced any complaints about her parents' betrayals or the hardships of her early years.

Although she was willing to let go of the past, she was adamant that my childhood would not be like hers. She began by saying my name. Xhosa families always give their children names that have a deeper significance, and such meanings tend to become self-fulfilling. You have Mlungisi, "The Fixer," my cousin. He is that person. He was the one who always tried to help me get out of trouble. He was always the kind kid, helping out around the family and performing housework. You have Velile, my uncle, and the unintended pregnancy. "The Person Who Suddenly Appeared" And he has only ever vanished and then reappeared throughout his existence. After going on a drinking binge, he will suddenly return a week later.

Patricia Nombuyiselo Noah, my mother, comes next. "She Who Returns the Favor." She does just that. She keeps giving and giving. Even as a young girl in Soweto, she did it. She would see toddlers, ages three and four, playing on the streets and running around unattended all day. Their mothers were alcoholics, and their fathers had disappeared. My mother, who was only six or seven years old at the time, would gather the stray children, organize a platoon, and transport them to the shebeens. The males who were passed out would give them their empties, and they would take the bottles to a location where you could drop them. With that money, my mom would then buy food from the spaza stores and feed the children. She was a kid looking after kids.

When it came time to choose my name, mother went with Trevor, which has no significance in South Africa and no family history. The name isn't even found in the Bible. It's only a name. My mother wished for her child to have no fate. She wanted me to be able to accomplish anything, be anyone, and go anywhere.

She also provided me with the means to accomplish it. I learned English as my first language from her. She was always reading to me. The book was the first book I ever learned to read. The Bible. We also obtained the majority of our other books from church. My mother would bring boxes filled with picture books, chapter books, and every other book she could find donated by white people home. After that, she joined a subscription service that sent us books via mail. The books were a set of how-to guides. A Guide to Effective Friendship. How to Be Truthful. She also purchased a collection of encyclopedias, which I would sit and go through even though they were fifteen years old and completely outdated.

My most valuable belongings were my books. I was really proud of the bookcase I had where I kept them. I maintained my books in immaculate condition because I liked them. I read them repeatedly without bending the pages or the spines. I loved each and every one of them. As I became older, I began purchasing books on my own. I cherished fantasy and enjoyed losing myself in imaginary worlds. I recall reading about white lads who solved mysteries or other such things. I didn't have time for that. Roald Dahl, please. The BFG, Charlie and the Chocolate Factory, James and the Giant Peach, and The Wonderful Story of Henry Sugar. My fix was that.
I fought to get my mother to buy me the Narnia novels. They didn't appeal to her.

She declared, "This lion is a false idol—a counterfeit God! You recall what transpired after Moses received the tablets and descended from the mountain?
"Yes, Mom," I clarified, "but the lion is a representation of Christ. He is, in a sense, Jesus. It is a narrative that explains Jesus.
That didn't sit well with her. "No, no. My friend, don't worship false idols.
I eventually got the better of her. It was a significant victory.
My mother wanted to unleash my thoughts, if she had any purpose. It was unusual for my mother to talk to me like an adult. In South Africa, adults converse with adults and children play with children. Although the adults watch over you, they don't approach you or engage in conversation. My mother did. Always. I resembled her closest friend. She never stopped teaching me, especially Bible lessons, and sharing stories with me. She loved the Psalms. Every day I had to read the Psalms. She'd test me on it. What is meant by the passage? For you, what does it mean? How do you use it in your daily life? Every day of my life was like that. What the school did

not do, my mom did. I learned how to think from her.

Apartheid was gradually abolished. It wasn't like the Berlin Wall, which fell all at once. Over many years, the walls of apartheid weakened and cracked. Some laws were repealed, some concessions were made here and there, and some were just not enforced. We were able to live less covertly in the months leading up to Mandela's release. My mother made the decision that we had to relocate at that point. She believed that we had developed as much as we could while hiding in our small town apartment.

On the East Rand, Eden Park was a colored community that was close to a number of black townships. Like us, she thought, half-black, half-colored. There, we would blend in. We never fit in at all; it didn't work out that way. However, when we made the move, she was thinking that. It was also an opportunity to purchase a house—our own house. One of those "suburbs" that is truly on the outskirts of civilization is Eden Park, the type of area where real estate developers have said, "Hey, poor people." You too can lead a fulfilling life. This is a home. In the midst of nothingness. You have a yard, though! The streets in Eden Park were given vehicle names for whatever reason: Jaguar Street. Ferrari Street. Honda Street. I'm not sure if that was a coincidence, but it's funny considering South Africans of color are known for their love of expensive cars. Every street was named after a great wine variety, making it feel like you were living in a white community.

We eventually obtained a car when we moved to Eden Park; it was a tangerine, beat-up Volkswagen that my mother had purchased used for almost nothing. It would not start one in five times. No air conditioning was present. Every time I accidentally turned on the fan, dust and leaf fragments would be flung all over me via the vent. We would catch minibuses whenever it broke down, or occasionally we would hitchhike. Knowing that men would stop for a woman but not a woman with a child, she would force me to hide in the bushes. I would rush up to the car after she stood by the road, the driver would stop, she would open the door, and then she would whistle. When they discovered they were picking up a pretty single woman with a big little child instead of a pretty single woman, I would see their faces fall.

We were frying in the heat and sputtering along with the windows down when the car finally started up. The radio dial in the car remained on the same station for the entirety of my life. It was named Radio Pulpit, and it was only praise and sermons, as the name implies. That dial was off limits to me. My mother would play a cassette of Jimmy Swaggart sermons whenever the radio was unreachable.

Even if our car was a car, it was still a car. It was liberty. We weren't Black people waiting for public transportation in the townships. We were out in the world as Black people. "Where do we choose to go today?" was a question we Black people could ask ourselves as we woke up. There was a lengthy section of the road into town that was totally empty on the way to work and school. Mom would let me drive there. on the freeway. I was six years old. While she operated the pedals and stick shift, she would place me on her lap and let me steer and use the indicators. She showed me how to work the stick after a few months of that. She was still working the clutch, but I'd climb onto her lap and take the stick, and she'd call out the gears as we drove. One stretch of the road traveled deep into a valley before climbing back up the opposite side. We'd get up a head of speed, and we'd stick it into neutral and let go of the brake and the clutch, and, woo-hoo!, we'd race down the hill and then, zoom!, we'd shoot up the other side. We were in the air.

Food, or the availability of food, has always been a gauge of how well or poorly our lives are going. "My job is to feed your body, feed your spirit, and feed your mind," my mother would often say. She spent nothing at all on anything else in order to find the money for food and books, and that's exactly what she did. She was legendary for being thrifty. We lived in the middle of nowhere, and our car was a tin can on wheels. We had broken old sofas with holes in the fabric and tattered furniture. We had a small black-and-white television with a rabbit aerial. The buttons weren't working, so we used a pair of pliers to change the stations. You had to squint most of the time to see what was happening.

We always wore used clothing that was either given to us by white people at church or from Goodwill stores. Every other student in school had Adidas and Nike labels. I never had any brands. I once requested Adidas sneakers from my mother. She brought some Abidas knockoffs home with her.

I said, "Mom, these are fake."

"I fail to see the distinction."

Take a look at the logo. Instead of three stripes, there are four.

"You're lucky," she said. "You have an extra one."

We survived on almost nothing, but we always had food, books, and religion. It wasn't particularly good food, mind you. Meat was considered a luxury. We would eat chicken when everything was going great. When it came to removing the last of the marrow from a chicken bone, my mother was an adept. We did not consume chicken. We wiped them out. An archaeologist's worst nightmare was our family. We didn't leave any bones. Only the head remained after we finished eating a bird. At times, the only meat we had was "sawdust," a packed beef that you could get from the butcher. It was actually the meat dust, the pieces that dropped off the cuts that were being packaged for the store, the fat fragments, and whatever was left over. After sweeping it up, they would place it in bags. My mother purchased it for us even though it was intended for dogs. We ate nothing but that for several months.

I never felt impoverished despite the humble lifestyle we led at home because we had so many experiences. We were constantly on the go, doing something. My mother used to drive me around affluent white communities. We would visit people's homes and take in their palaces. Since that was all we could see from the road, we would primarily gaze at their walls. We would say, "Wow," when we saw a wall that extended from one end of the block to the other. It's just one house. That is all for a single household. She would occasionally place me on her shoulders like I was a tiny periscope when we pulled over and approached the wall. I would describe what I saw as I peered into the yards. The house is large and white! They have two canines! A lemon tree is present! There's a pool there! A tennis court, too!

Black people never went to the places my mother took me to. She resisted being constrained by absurd notions of what Black people should or cannot accomplish. She would take me skating at the ice rink. On top of a huge mine dump outside the city, Johannesburg once had the famous Top Star Drive-In drive-in theater. There, she would drive me to see movies; we would grab some snacks and mount the speaker on the windshield of our automobile. Top Star offered a full 360-degree view of Soweto, the suburbs, and the city. I could see for miles in all directions up there. The world seemed to be on top of me.

We encourage individuals to pursue their ambitions, but you can only dream of what you can envision, and your imagination may be fairly constrained depending on your background. Our dream as children in Soweto was to add a room to our home. Have a driveway, perhaps. Perhaps a cast-iron gate at the driveway's terminus one day. Because we only knew that. However, the pinnacle of what is feasible is well beyond your visible reality. I was shown what was possible by my mother. I was constantly in awe of her life since no one ever showed her. Nobody picked her. It was her own doing. By pure willpower, she managed to find her way.

People said my mother was insane. Suburban areas, drive-ins, and ice rinks were all considered izinto zabelungu, or white people's property. The ideology of apartheid had been internalized and adopted by a large number of Black people. Why teach white things to a black child? My mother used to be harassed by neighbors and family. "Why all of this? Since he will never leave the ghetto, why show him the world?
"Because," she would explain, "he will understand that the ghetto is not the world, even if he never leaves it." I have done enough if that is all I manage to do.

Chapter 6: Loopholes

"I chose to have you because I wanted something to love and something that would love me unconditionally in return—and then I gave birth to the most selfish piece of shit on earth and all it ever did was cry and eat and shit and say, 'Me, me, me, me me,'" my mother used to say to me.

I was also hyperactive. I yearned for continual activity and excitement. If you didn't had my arm in a deadly grasp when I was a child, I would have raced straight for the traffic as I went down the sidewalk. I enjoyed being pursued. I mistook it for a game. The elderly grandmothers my mother employed to watch me while she was at work? I would weep when I left them. They would be crying when my mom got home. "I give up. I am unable to do this. A tyrant is your son. The same applied to the Sunday school teachers and my own teachers. You were in trouble if you weren't talking to me. People didn't think I was a shit. I wasn't spoiled or whiny. I was polite. I simply had a lot of enthusiasm and knew what I wanted to accomplish.

In order to burn off the energy, my mom would take me to the park and run me till I died. She would toss a Frisbee, and I would run after it, catch it, and return it. Again and again. She would occasionally toss a tennis ball. Dogs owned by Black people don't play fetch; you only toss food to a Black person's dog. I didn't understand my mom was training me like a dog until I started hanging out in parks with white folks and their pets.

Knives and fire were my two favorite things. I couldn't get enough of them. Simply put, knives were cool. I gathered flick knives, butterfly knives, the Rambo knife, and the Crocodile Dundee knife from pawnshops and yard sales. But the final was fire. I had a deep affection for fire, and fireworks in particular. Every year, my mom would buy us a mini-arsenal of pyrotechnics to mark Guy Fawkes Day in November. I came to the realization that I could make my own enormous firework by extracting the gunpowder from each of the pyrotechnics. I got sidetracked by some Black Cat firecrackers one afternoon while playing with my cousin and filling an empty plant pot with a massive quantity of gunpowder. One of the fun things about a Black Cat was that you could break it in two and ignite it to make it a miniature flamethrower, rather than lighting it to have it explode. I accidentally put a match into my gunpowder pile when I paused in the middle of building it to play with the Black Cats. A huge ball of flame erupted in my face as the entire thing exploded. My mother rushed into the yard in a panic as Mlungisi wailed.

"What took place?!"
I could still feel the fireball's heat on my face, but I pretended not to be bothered. "Oh, nothing. Nothing took place.
"Did you try to play with fire?"
"No."
She gave a headshake. "You know what? Jesus has already exposed your falsehoods, but I would still beat you.
"What?"
"Look at yourself in the restroom."
I looked in the mirror after using the restroom. The front inch or so of my hair was entirely burned out, and my eyebrows were gone.
When I was younger, I didn't think of myself as destructive and uncontrollable, but as an adult, I did. I had no desire to destroy. I desired to produce. I didn't have my eyebrows burning. I was starting a fire. Overhead projectors weren't being broken by me. I was causing mayhem in order to observe how people responded. And I was powerless to stop it. Children with compulsive disorder have a condition that causes them to do things they don't comprehend. "Whatever you do, don't draw on the wall," is something you can say to a child. This paper is yours to draw on. This book allows you to draw. Any surface can be used for drawing. However, avoid writing,

coloring, or drawing on the wall. The child will say, "Got it," while staring you in the eye. The child is sketching on the wall ten minutes later. You scream. "What on earth are you doing drawing on the wall?" As he stares at you, the child honestly doesn't know why he drew on the wall. I recall experiencing that feeling constantly as a child. Every time I was disciplined, I would ask myself, "Why did I just do that?" while my mother was slapping my ass. I was aware that I shouldn't. I was advised not to do that by her. I would then tell myself, "I'm going to be so good from here on," after the hiding was over. I promise never to do anything terrible in my life. Let me write a reminder to myself on the wall to help me remember not to do anything bad. and then, for no apparent reason, I would pick up a crayon and immediately return to it.

She modified her strategy when I was seven or eight years old because I was too intelligent to be duped. Our lives became a courtroom drama as two attorneys argued about technicalities and loopholes all the time. I was quicker in an argument than my mother, who was intelligent and had a keen tongue. She would become agitated due to her inability to keep up. She then began to correspond with me. She could then argue her views without having to engage in back-and-forth verbal combat. When I got home from doing chores, I would discover an envelope— possibly from the landlord—slipped beneath the door.

I would take the letter to her and wait for her to finish reading it. She would always rip it up and dispose of it in the trash can. "Cheap! This is garbage! I would then respond, "Ah-ah-ah," as she began to fling herself at me. No. You must compose a letter. I would then retire to my room and await her response. At times, this fluctuated over several days.

My mother never left me wondering why I was getting the hiding, which was something I admired about her. It wasn't anger or fury. The discipline came from a loving place. My mom had a strange child and was on her own. I ruined pianos. I threw up on floors. She would beat the living daylights out of me, let me cry, and then return to my room with a broad smile and ask, "Are you ready for dinner? If we wish to watch Rescue 911, we must eat quickly. Will you be arriving?

"What? Are you some sort of psychopath? You just defeated me! Indeed. since you made a mistake. It doesn't imply that I no longer love you.

"What?"

"Look, did you do something wrong or not?"

"Yes, I did."

"Then? I struck you. And that's over now. Why sit there and weep, then? It's Rescue 911 time. Waiting is William Shatner. Will you be attending?

Catholic school was serious business when it came to discipline. The nuns at Maryvale used the edge of a metal ruler to slap me on the knuckles whenever I got into problems with them. They would use soap to clean my mouth for swearing. I would be taken to the principal's office for significant infractions. You could only get an official hiding from the principal. He would strike your ass with a flat rubber object, like to a shoe sole, requiring you to stoop.

It seemed like the principal was scared to strike me too hard every time. I started laughing when I thought, "Man, if only my mom hit me like this," as I was being reprimanded one day. I was unable to resist. The principal was agitated. Something is clearly wrong with you, he replied, "if you're laughing while you're being beaten."

That was the first of three occasions my mother was required to take me to a psychologist for an evaluation by the school. All of the psychologists who evaluated me said that there was nothing wrong with the child. I wasn't ADD. A sociopath is not what I was. I was simply energetic, inventive, and self-reliant. I did take a number of tests from the therapists, and they concluded that because I could constantly discover legal loopholes, I would either make a great criminal or be extremely successful at apprehending criminals. If a rule didn't make sense to me, I would figure out a method to get around it.

Since the rules didn't make sense, I didn't think I was breaking them. And they broke their own regulations, which is the only reason I was caught. I was turned in by the priest after another child caught me in confession.

"No, no," I argued. "You've disregarded the rules. That information is private. What you say in confession is not meant to be repeated by the priest.

They were indifferent. The school was free to disregard any regulations. I was scolded by the principal.

"What sort of sick person would consume all of Jesus's blood and eat all of his body?"

"A person who is hungry."

For that one, I received a second beating and a second visit to the psychologist. In sixth grade, the final straw was the third trip to the shrink. I was being bullied by a child. I brought one of my knives to school, and he threatened to bash me up. I merely wanted it; I had no intention of using it. The school was unconcerned. For them, that was the final straw. I wasn't really expelled. "We can expel you, Trevor," the principal stated after sitting me down. You must carefully consider if you truly wish to attend Maryvale the next year. He probably believed that by issuing me an ultimatum, I would change my ways. However, I thought he was giving me a way out, so I accepted it. I said to him, "No, I don't want to be here." Catholic education came to an end at that point.

Ironically, I avoided conflict with my mother at the time. At home, there was no ass-whooping for me. When she quit her work at ICI, she lost the bursary, and she was finding it difficult to pay for private education. More than that, though, she believed the school was exaggerating. In actuality, she most likely sided with me against Maryvale. Regarding the Eucharist, she completely agreed with me. She said to the principal, "Let me clarify this." "You're punishing a child because he desires the blood and flesh of Jesus? Why is he not entitled to such items? He ought to have them, of course. She informed the school it was also absurd when they forced me to see a therapist for laughing when the principal struck me.

"Your son was laughing while we were hitting him, Ms. Noah."

You obviously don't know how to beat a child. It's not my problem; it's yours. I can assure you that Trevor has never laughed when I have struck him.

That was my mother's peculiar and somewhat wonderful quality. She wouldn't discipline me for disobeying a rule if she thought it was foolish. She and the psychologists both agreed that the issue was not with me, but rather with the school. Being autonomous and creative is not appropriate in a Catholic school setting.

I was too young to understand who my mother and her new lover, Abel, were to one another when I was seven years old, but they had been dating for perhaps a year. "Hey, that's mom's friend who's around a lot," was all that was said. Abel was a genuinely kind person, and I liked him.

Every time we visited, I would play with her son. This white family also had a black maid who resided in the servants' quarters in the backyard. My passion for fire was at its peak at that age. My mom, Abel, and both of the white parents were at work one afternoon when the child and I were playing together while his mother was cleaning the house. Using a magnifying lens to burn my name into wood pieces was one of my favorite pastimes at the time. Before you could burn shapes, characters, and patterns, you had to orient the lens, get the focus exactly so, and then move the flame carefully. It captivated me.

I was showing this child how to do it that afternoon. We entered the servants' quarters, which were actually an addition to the back of the house that resembled a toolshed and was furnished with turpentine, buckets of old paint, and wooden ladders. Along with all of my standard fire-making supplies, I also brought a box of matches. We were seated on an ancient mattress—basically, a bag filled with dried straw—that they had previously used to sleep on the floor. I was demonstrating to the child how to burn his name onto a piece of plywood while the sun shone through the window.

We stopped at one point to grab a snack. We departed after I placed the matches and magnifying lens on the mattress. We discovered the shed had one of those doors that self-locks from the inside when we returned a short while later. We chose to play and run around in the yard since we couldn't return inside without going to fetch his mother. After some time, I saw smoke emerging from the window frame's crevices. I rushed over and had a look inside. We had left the matches and the magnifying lens on the straw mattress, and in the center of the mattress was a little fire. We summoned the maid and ran. She arrived, but she was unsure of what to do. The door was locked, and everything caught—the ladders, the paint, the turpentine, the mattress—before we could find out how to enter the shed.

The fire spread swiftly. Before long, the entire house was engulfed in flames, starting with the roof and spreading to the main house. There was smoke rising into the air. The sirens were on their way after a neighbor alerted the fire department. I hurried out to the road with this child and the maid to see the firefighters attempt to extinguish it, but it was already too late. Only a burnt brick and mortar shell, with the roof gone and the interior gutted, remained.

After returning home, the white family stood in the street and gazed at the wreckage of their home. When the maid was asked what had happened, she asked her son, and the child was completely taken aback. He said, "Trevor had matches." I heard nothing from the family. They probably didn't know what to say. They were utterly bewildered. They didn't threaten to sue or contact the police. Arresting a seven-year-old for arson was their only option. Furthermore, you couldn't really sue us for anything since we were so impoverished. That was the end of it because they also had insurance.

Since the freestanding garage was the only part of the property that remained intact, I found it amusing that they ejected Abel from it. They forced Abel to leave, even though I didn't see why he should. Abel essentially moved in with us after we packed up his belongings, loaded them into our car, and went home to Eden Park. He got into a heated argument with my mother. "My life has been destroyed by your son!" However, I was not punished that day. My mother was too shocked. There is mischievous behavior and then setting a white person's home on fire. She was unsure about what to do.

I didn't feel guilty about it. I haven't yet. I am totally innocent, according to the lawyer in me. There was a mattress, matches, and a magnifying glass, and then obviously a string of bad things happened. Sometimes things catch fire. The fire department exists for this reason. However, everyone in my family will tell you that "a house was burned down by Trevor." I was notorious after the fire, if people thought I was nasty before. I was no longer called Trevor by one of my uncles. Instead, he referred to me as "Terror." He would remark,

"Don't leave that child alone in your house." "He's going to burn it down."

Even now, my cousin Mlungisi still finds it hard to understand how I managed to stay as mischievous as I was for as long as I did and how I endured the numerous hidings I received. Why did my misbehavior persist? Why didn't I learn my lesson sooner? My cousins were both excellent children. Mlungisi may be hiding something in his life. He then declared that he would never want to go through anything similar again, and he started abiding by the regulations after that. However, I was also fortunate to inherit my mother's gift of forgetting life's hardships. Although I can recall the event that led to the trauma, I don't dwell on it. I never allowed the recollection of a terrible experience stop me from attempting anything new. You will cease pushing the boundaries and breaking the rules if you dwell too much on the ass-kicking you received from your mother or from life in general. It's better to accept it, cry for a while, then get up the next day and go on. It's acceptable that you will have some bruises to serve as a reminder of what transpired. The bruises eventually go away, though, and with good reason—it's time to get up to some crap again.

Chapter 7: Fufi

My mother brought home two cats a month after we relocated to Eden Park. Black cats. Lovely animals. My mom ended up with two of the kittens from a litter of kittens that a woman at her workplace was attempting to get rid of. I had never owned a pet before, so I was thrilled. My mother, who adores animals, was thrilled. She didn't think there was any cat-related nonsense. She was defying expectations of what Black people should and shouldn't do, which was simply another example of her rebellious behavior.

In Soweto, we had never owned pets. Then one day we were offered two puppies by a woman at my mom's workplace. They weren't supposed to be pups. The bull terrier from next door had impregnated this woman's Maltese poodle, creating an odd hybrid. My mother promised to take them both. I was the happiest child alive when she brought them home. My mother gave them the names Panther and Fufi. Fufi.

Fufi was my dog, and Panther was my mom's. Fufi was stunning. Happy face, neat lines. Despite being skinnier due to the Maltese mixed in, she had the appearance of a perfect bull terrier. Panther, who was more half-and-half, appeared strange and disheveled. Panther was intelligent. Fufi was a complete moron. We always assumed she was stupid, at least. Panther would arrive as soon as we summoned them, but Fufi would do nothing. After Panther ran back to fetch Fufi, they would both arrive. As it happened, Fufi was deaf. Years later, while a burglar was attempting to enter our home, Fufi passed away. She shattered her spine when the fence fell on her back after he pushed it over. She had to be put down when we took her to the veterinarian. The veterinarian came over and gave us the news after evaluating her.

He remarked, "Your family must have found it odd to have a deaf dog."

"What?"

"You were unaware that your dog was deaf?"

"No, we believed it to be foolish."

It dawned on us then that one dog had been giving the other instructions in some way for their entire lives. The hearing, intelligent one was assisting the deaf, stupid one.

My life's love was Fufi. Lovely but foolish. She was reared by me. She was potty-trained by me. My bed was where she slept. Having a dog is a wonderful gift for children. It's similar to a bicycle, but emotional.

Fufi was capable of many stunts. She had a really high jumping ability. Fufi could jump, after all. She would jump up and catch a piece of food I held up above her head as if it were nothing. Fufi would have been well-known if YouTube had existed.

Fufi was also a bit of a miscreant. We kept the dogs in the backyard during the day, which was surrounded by a wall that was at least five feet high. After a time, Fufi would be waiting for us outside the gate each day when we returned home. We were perpetually perplexed. Was the gate being opened? What was happening? We had never considered that she was capable of scaling a five-foot wall, yet that was precisely what was taking place. Fufi would wait for us to leave each morning, then leap over the wall and wander the neighborhood.

When I was at home during the school break, I managed to catch her one day. I was in the living room when my mother departed for work. Because the automobile was gone, Fufi assumed I was gone and was unaware that I was present. When I looked outside after hearing Panther barking in the backyard, I saw Fufi climbing the wall. She had leaped, scrambled up the final few feet, and vanished.

It was unbelievable to me that this was taking place. I sprinted outside, picked up my bike, and followed her to find out her destination. She traveled to a different area of the neighborhood, many blocks away. Next she approached another house, leaped over their wall, and entered their backyard. How on earth was she doing this? I rang the doorbell as I approached the gate. This child of color responded.

"Can I assist you?" he asked.

Indeed. You have my dog in your yard.

"What?"

"My canine companion. You have her in your yard.

Fufi approached and placed himself between us.

"Come, Fufi!" I exclaimed. "Come on!"

This child referred to Fufi by some other dumb nickname, such as Spotty or anything like, after glancing at her.

"Return inside the house, Spotty."

I exclaimed, "Whoa, whoa." "Spotty? That's Fufi!

"No, that's Spotty, my dog."

"No, that's my friend Fufi."

"No, it's Spotty here."

How could Spotty be involved? She has no spots at all. You have no idea what you're discussing.

"This is Spotty!"

"Fufi!"

"Spotty!"

"Fufi!"

Naturally, Fufi did not answer to "Spotty" or "Fufi" because she was deaf. She remained still. I began to curse the child.

"Return my dog to me!"

He answered, "I don't know who you are, but you had better leave."

After that, he walked inside to fetch his mother, who emerged.

She asked, "What do you want?"

"My dog is that!"

"This is our canine. Leave.

I burst into tears. "Why are you taking my dog away from me?" I turned and pleaded with Fufi. "Why are you treating me like this, Fufi? Fufi, why? Why? I gave her a call. I pleaded with her to attend. I begged Fufi, but he was deaf. and anything else.

With tears streaming down my cheeks, I hopped on my bike and rode quickly home. I was a huge fan of Fufi. I reared her, and after all the nights we spent together, it was shocking to see her with another boy, pretending she didn't know me. I was devastated.

Fufi didn't come home that night. The other household locked her inside because they believed I was coming to take their dog, making it impossible for her to return to wait for us outside the fence as she always did. My mother returned home from her job. I was crying. I informed her that Fufi had been abducted. We returned to the residence. My mother confronted the mother after ringing the bell.

"This is our dog, you see."

My mother was deceived by this woman. "This dog is not yours. This dog was purchased by us.

"The puppy wasn't purchased by you. Our dog is it.

They walked back and forth. Since this woman wouldn't budge, we went home to gather proof, including photos of us with the dogs and veterinarian certifications. My mother was getting impatient with me since I was crying the entire time. "Stop shedding tears! We'll pick up the dog! Relax!

After gathering our paperwork, we returned to the house. As part of the evidence, we took Panther along this time. My mother showed this woman the veterinarian's information and photos. She refused to give us Fufi even now. My mother threatened to contact law enforcement. It became an entire thing. My mother finally said, "All right, I'll give you a hundred rand."

"All right," the woman said.

She brought Fufi out after my mom handed her some cash. The second child had to see his mother sell the dog he believed to be his since he believed Fufi to be Spotty. He began to cry now. "Spotty! No! You can't sell Spotty, Mom! I didn't give a damn. I only desired the return of Fufi.

Fufi arrived as soon as she noticed Panther. We went for a walk with the dogs. Still heartbroken, I cried all the way home. Mom didn't have time to listen to my complaints.

"What's causing your tears?"

"Because Fufi has feelings for another boy."

"All right? Why would you be hurt by that? You didn't pay anything for it. Fufi is present. She still has feelings for you. You still own her. Therefore, go on.

My first heartbreak was with Fufi. Fufi has betrayed me more than anyone else has. For me, it was a worthwhile lesson. Realizing that Fufi wasn't having an affair with another boy was difficult. She was just making the most of her existence. Her previous relationship hadn't had any impact on me until I found out that she was going out alone during the day. Fufi was not malevolent.

Naturally, I was mistaken to think that Fufi was my dog. Fufi was a canine. I was a boy. We had a good relationship. She was a resident of my home. I have felt this way about relationships ever since that experience: You do not own what you love. I was fortunate to have learned that lesson so early in life. Even as adults, a lot of my friends still struggle with emotions of betrayal. I sympathize with them when they come to me in tears and anger, telling me how they have been deceived and cheated on. I can relate to what they're experiencing. I get them a drink, sit down with them, and tell them, "Friend, let me tell you the story of Fufi."

Chapter 8: Robert

I have no idea who my father is. I still don't have the answers to all the questions that surround his life.

Where did he grow up? Switzerland, somewhere.

Where did he attend college? If he did, I'm not sure.

What brought him to South Africa? I don't know.

My grandparents are Swiss, but I've never met them. I don't know anything about them, not even their names. Although I've never met her, I am aware that my dad has an older sister. I am aware that he spent some time working as a chef in New York and Montreal before relocating to South Africa in the late 1970s. I am aware that he was employed by an industrial food service company and that he occasionally established restaurants and bars. That's all.

I never referred to my father as "Dad." I also never called him "Daddy" or "Father." I was unable to. I was told not to. People might have overheard us if I called him "Dad" in public or anywhere else, and they might have questioned us or called the police. I have therefore always named him Robert for as long as I can remember.

He never got married, as far as I know. He used to declare that he never wanted to be controlled and that most people marry to control someone else. I am aware that he enjoys entertaining, traveling, and hosting guests. However, he values his solitude above all else. He never appears in the phone book, no matter where he resides. If he hadn't been so private, I'm sure my parents would have been caught during their time together. My mother was erratic and impetuous. My dad was quiet and sensible. He was ice and she was fire. I am a combination of both of them; they were opposites that drew each other in.

I do know one thing about my dad: he detests bigotry and homogeneity above all else, and not because he feels morally superior or self-righteous. He simply couldn't comprehend how bigoted white people might be in South Africa. He would reply, "Africa is full of Black people." If you despise Black people, why would you travel all the way to Africa? Why did you move into their home if you had such a strong dislike for Black people? It seemed crazy to him.

My father never believed in any of the apartheid laws because racism never made sense to him. He launched a steakhouse, one of Johannesburg's first integrated restaurants, in the early 1980s, before I was even born. In order to enable enterprises to service both Black and white customers, he asked for a special license. Black South Africans with money took advantage of this loophole to frequent the hotels and restaurants that required these licenses in order to serve black tourists and diplomats from other nations, who were theoretically exempt from the same restrictions as black South Africans.

My dad's restaurant was a huge success right away. Black people came because they wanted to sit in a fine restaurant and experience what it was like, and there weren't many high-end places where they could eat. In order to experience what it was like to sit among Black people, white people attended. Black people would sit and eat while the white people watched them eat, and the white people would sit and watch the black people eat. The desire to be together outweighed the hostility that kept individuals apart. The atmosphere was fantastic.

Only because a few locals took it upon themselves to voice their displeasure did the eatery close. The authorities began looking for methods to shut down my dad once they filed petitions. When the inspectors first arrived, they attempted to discipline him for infractions of the health and cleanliness codes. It was obvious that they were unfamiliar with the Swiss. That was a colossal failure. They then made the decision to target him by enforcing more capricious limitations.

They stated, "You can continue to operate the restaurant since you

e, but you will need to have separate restrooms for each
White toilets, black toilets, colored toilets, and Indian
necessary.
at, the entire restaurant will consist of just restrooms."
alternative is to turn it into a regular restaurant that serves
eople if you don't want to do that."
He shut down the eatery.

Following the end of apartheid, my father relocated from Hillbrow to Yeoville, a once peaceful residential area that had become a multicultural melting pot of black, white, and every other color. With their diverse cuisine and lively music, immigrants were flooding in from Ghana, Nigeria, and other parts of the continent. The main strip, Rockey Street, has taverns, restaurants, and street merchants lining its sidewalks. It was a cultural eruption.

I liked going to this amazing park on Yeo Street, where my dad resided, two blocks over from Rockey. Children of all races and nationalities were playing and running around. My dad had a modest home. Nice, although not too elaborate. Although he never made extravagant purchases, I believe my dad had enough money to travel and live comfortably. He is a very frugal man who has been driving the same vehicle for twenty years.

I followed a schedule with my father. Every Sunday afternoon, I went to see him. Despite the end of apartheid, my mother had already decided she didn't want to marry. Consequently, he had his house and we had ours. Together, my mom and I had agreed that if I accompanied her to mixed and white churches in the morning, I would be allowed to skip black church and go to my dad's, where we would watch Formula 1 racing rather than cast out demons.

All we had were Sunday afternoons, except for special events and birthdays. He would prepare meals for me. He would ask me what I wanted to eat, and I would always say the same thing: Rösti, a German pancake cooked with potatoes and sauce and some kind of meat. That, a bottle of Sprite, and a plastic container of custard with caramel on top for dessert are what I'd have.

Many of those afternoons were spent in quiet. My father was reticent.

He was loving, loyal, and meticulous. He always sent me a letter on my birthday and brought my favorite foods and toys whenever I visited. However, he was a secret at the same time. We would discuss the meals he was preparing and the Formula One races we had witnessed. Occasionally, he would provide a bit of information about his steakhouse or a place he had been to. But that was all. It was like watching a web series when I was with my dad. I would have to wait a week for the next installment after receiving a few minutes of information at a time.

My dad went to Cape Town when I was thirteen, and we lost contact. There were two reasons why we had been drifting apart for some time. I was a teenager. I was suddenly dealing with a completely other environment. For me, playing video games and using computers were more important than seeing my parents. My mother had also wed Abel. As my mom had done back in Hillbrow, I progressed from seeing my dad every Sunday to seeing him every other Sunday, maybe once a month, whenever she could smuggle me over. After experiencing apartheid, we were now subject to a different form of tyranny—that of an alcoholic and violent guy.

At the same time, Yeoville began to experience widespread decay, neglect, and white flight. The majority of my dad's German pals had moved to Cape Town. He went as he had no incentive to stay if he wasn't seeing me. I thought it was just Dad's temporary relocation to Cape Town. Then he vanished. I continued to remain busy with my life, making it through high school, getting through my early twenties, and becoming a comedian. My career went off in no time. I presented a kids' adventure reality show on television and landed a job as a radio DJ. I was performing as the main act in clubs around the nation. However, even as my life progressed, the concerns I had about my father continued to linger in the back of my mind and occasionally surface. Could you tell me where he is? Is he considering me? Is he aware of what I'm doing? Is he pleased with me? You're left in the dark when a parent isn't there, and it's really simple to think negatively during that time. "They don't give a damn." "They are self-centered." The fact that my mother never said anything negative about him was my only hope. She was continuously praising him. "You manage your finances well. Your father is the source of that. "Your dad's smile is in you." "You're as neat and orderly as your dad." She made sure I understood that his absence was due to circumstances rather than a lack of affection, so I never became resentful. Every time she came home from the hospital, she would tell me the story of my dad asking, "Where's my kid? That child is someone I want in my life. She would tell me, "Remember that He picked you." And in the end, my mother forced me to find him when I reached twenty-four.

Since my father is not listed on my birth certificate, I had no evidence that he was my father when I wrote to the Swiss embassy to ask where he was. In response, the embassy stated that they were unable to provide me with any information since they were unsure of my identity. They also gave me the runaround when I tried to phone them. They said, "Look, kid." "We are unable to assist you. We are the embassy of Switzerland. Are you ignorant of the Swiss? We are something of a discretionary bunch. That's what we do. Bad luck. I persisted in nagging them until they finally replied, "All right, we'll take your letter and we might forward it to a man like the one you're describing if he exists." Perhaps we won't if he doesn't. Let's observe what occurs.

A note that read, "Great to hear from you," arrived in the mail a few months later. How are you? Dad, love. A few months after he gave me his address, I went to see him in Cape Town, in the Camps Bay suburb.

I will always remember that day. Meeting someone I knew but did not know at all was perhaps one of the most strange days of my life. My recollections of him seemed elusive. I was attempting to recall his mannerisms, his laughter, and his speech patterns. After parking on his street, I began to search for his address. There are a lot of older, semiretired white folks in Camps Bay, and while I was walking down the road, I saw a lot of these elderly white men passing by and approaching me. By then, my father was in his seventies, and I was terrified that I had forgotten his appearance. Every time an elderly white man passed me, I looked him in the face and asked, "Are you my daddy?" In essence, it appeared as though I was cruising elderly white males in a retirement community by the sea. When I eventually arrived at the address I had been given, I rang the bell and recognized him as soon as he answered the door. Hello! I assumed it was you. It's you, of course. You're the one. You are someone I know.

We continued where we had left off, with his treating me in the same manner that he had when I was thirteen. My father immediately re-entered it, like the habitual person he was. "All right! Where were we, then? I have all of your favorites right here. Rösti of potatoes. Sprite in a bottle. caramelized custard. Fortunately, I jumped right in because my tastes hadn't changed much since I was thirteen.

He got up while I was eating and returned to the table with this book and an enormous photo album. He opened it and said, "I've been following you." From the start of my career till that week, it was a scrapbook of everything I had ever done, from magazine covers to the smallest club listings, every time my name appeared in a newspaper. As he walked me through everything and showed me the headlines, he was grinning broadly. "This Saturday, Trevor Noah will be performing at the Blues Room." "A New TV Show Hosted by Trevor Noah"

I was overcome with a surge of emotions. I did everything in my power to keep from crying. It seemed like only a day had gone by since I'd last seen him, and the ten-year void in my life had suddenly closed. I had so many questions for years. Does he have me on his mind? Is he aware of what I'm doing? Is he pleased with me? However, he had been by my side the entire time. I had always made him proud. Even though circumstances had caused us to separate ways, he was always my father.

That day, I left his house a little taller. The sight of him had confirmed that he had picked me. I am the one he chose to have in his life. He decided to respond to my letter. They wanted me. The best gift you can give a human being is to be selected.

After we got back in touch, I felt compelled to make up for all the years we had lost. I concluded that interviewing him was the best course of action. That was a mistake that I quickly realized. You will get facts and information from interviews, but that wasn't really what I was looking for. An interview is not a connection, which is what I wanted. Silence is the foundation of relationships. Time is what apartheid took away from us; you spend time with people, observe and engage with them, and get to know them. An interview cannot make up for that, but I had to discover it for myself.

I made it my goal to get to know my father this weekend when I went down to spend a few days with him. I began asking him questions as soon as I got there. "Where are you from? What school did you attend? You did this, but why? How did you accomplish that? He began to show signs of irritation.

"What's this?" he inquired. "Why are you asking me questions? What is happening here?

"I'd like to learn more about you."

"Is questioning people how you typically get to know them?"

"Well, not really."

How do you meet new people, then?

"I'm not sure. I suppose by spending time with them.

"All right. Spend time with me, then. Check out what you discover.

Thus, we stayed together throughout the weekend. We discussed politics over supper. We discussed sports while watching Formula One racing. We listened to old Elvis Presley records while sitting peacefully in his lawn. He didn't mention himself once during the entire conversation. Then he approached me and sat down as I was getting ready to go.

"So, what do you think you've learned about your dad in the time we've spent together?" he said.

"Nothin'. I just know that you are very secretive.

"You see? You're already getting to know me.

Part II

An indigenous group known as the Khoisan was present when Dutch colonists arrived at the southern tip of Africa more than three hundred years ago. In contrast to the darker, Bantu-speaking peoples that eventually migrated south to become the Zulu, Xhosa, and Sotho tribes of modern-day South Africa, the Khoisan are the Native Americans of South Africa, a vanished tribe of bushmen, and nomadic hunter-gatherers. The first mixed people in South Africa were created when white colonists had their way with Khoisan women while they were settling in Cape Town and the adjacent frontier.

Slaves were quickly brought in from all across the Dutch empire, including Madagascar, the East Indies, and West Africa, to labor the colonists' crops. Over time, the Khoisan virtually vanished from South Africa as a result of the intermarriage between the slaves and the white colonists, as well as their constant dipping in and taking of their liberties. The last members of their family were bred extinct and combined with the offspring of whites and slaves to create a completely new race of people known as coloreds, while the majority were wiped off by disease, starvation, and conflict. People of color are a whole blend, a hybrid. Some are black, while others are light. Some people are black, some are white, and some have Asian traits. A child born to a colored woman and a colored man frequently doesn't resemble either parent at all.

Having no distinct heritage to return to is a curse that colored people bear. Their ancestry eventually divides into white and native and a complex network of "other" if they go back far enough. Their biggest bond has always been with their white fathers, the Afrikaners, as their native mothers are no longer with them. African languages are not spoken by the majority of people of color. They can communicate in Afrikaans. Afrikaners were the ones who created their institutions, their religion, and everything else that influenced their culture.

In this regard, the history of South Africans of color is worse than that of South Africans of black descent. Black people are aware of their identity because of all the hardships they have endured. People of color don't.

Chapter 9: The Mulberry Tree

There was a huge mulberry tree growing out of someone's front yard at the end of our street in Eden Park, precisely at the bend at the top of the road. When it produced fruit each year, the kids from the neighborhood would go pick berries from it, eat as many as they could, and pack bags to carry home. Together, they would play beneath the tree. I was left alone to play beneath the tree. Eden Park was a place where I had no friends.

One of the most difficult things I've ever experienced is the hostility I experienced from the people of color I came into contact with as a child. I learned that being an outsider as an insider is more difficult than being an insider as an outsider. Black people will respond, "Cool, white guy," if a white man decides to primarily associate with black people and immerse himself in hip-hop culture. Take care of your obligations. White people will respond, "All right," if a black man decides to hide his race in order to live with white people and play a lot of golf. Brian appeals to me. He is secure. However, imagine being a Black person who lives in the Black community while immersing himself in white society. Try living in a white town while embracing the accoutrements of black culture as a white person. You will experience more ostracism, mockery, and hate than you can ever imagine. If people perceive you as an outsider attempting to fit in, they are more likely to accept you. However, they will never forgive you if they perceive you as a fellow tribe member who is trying to betray the tribe. I had such experience in Eden Park.

Colored people were difficult to classify when apartheid arrived, so the regime cleverly exploited them to foment doubt, anger, and confusion. Colored individuals became the "near-whites" for state reasons. In order to keep them waiting for more, they were treated as second-class citizens, denied the rights of white people, but granted preferential treatment that black people did not. They were known as amperbaas, or "the almost-boss," in Afrikaans. The near-master. "You're nearly there. You're quite near. This is how close you are to being white. It's a shame your granddad couldn't resist eating the chocolate. But keep trying; it's not your fault that you're colored. Because this taint can be removed from your lineage if you put forth enough effort. Continue marrying whiter and lighter people, avoid touching the chocolate, and if you're lucky, you might one day turn white.

which seems absurd, but it would occur. During apartheid, some persons of color would be promoted to white positions every year. It was real; it wasn't a myth. The government would accept applications from the public. If your complexion lightens, your accent becomes polished, and your hair straightens sufficiently, you might be classed as white. All you needed to do was abandon your darker-skinned relatives and family, condemn your tribe, and denounce your past.

Additionally, persons of color weren't just promoted to white positions. Colored people can occasionally turn Indian. Indians occasionally become colorful. Colored people were occasionally downgraded to black, and black people were occasionally exalted to colored. Of course, white people may also be relegated to brown people. That was crucial. White people were kept in line by their fear of losing their standing, and those mixed lineages were always ready to show. Even if both parents provided documents demonstrating they were white, the child could be classed as colored if the government determined the child was too dark. In this case, the family would have to pick a choice. In order to live as colored people in a colored area, do they relinquish their white status? Or would they separate, the father remaining white to earn a living to support them while the mother took the brown child to live in the ghetto?

People of color had a difficult time. Consider the following scenario: You have been brainwashed into thinking that your blood is contaminated. All of your attention has been devoted to blending in and striving for whiteness. Then, just when you think you're almost done, a fucking man named Nelson Mandela shows up and completely changes the course of history. The benchmark is now black, and the finish line is once again where the beginning line was. Black is in command. Black is lovely. Black has strength. Black people are monkeys, colored people have been told for generations. Don't swing like them from the trees. Take up the white man's erect gait. Suddenly, the monkeys have seized over and it's Planet of the Apes.

It was strange for me, as you may guess. My complexion was colored, but not by culture; I was mixed but not colored. I was perceived as a colored person who didn't want to be colored as a result.

I saw two different kinds of people of color at Eden Park. I was loathed by some individuals of color because I was black. I was proud of my Afro and had curly hair. I enjoyed speaking the languages of Africa. When I spoke Zulu or Xhosa, people would ask, "What is jy? 'n Boesman?" "A Bushman, what are you?" You're striving to be Black, but why? You speak that click-click language, but why? Examine your pale complexion. You're discarding it even if you're almost there.

I wasn't liked, even when I believed I was. I once received a brand-new bike for the summer vacation. I was riding around the block with my cousin Mlungisi. When this adorable colored girl walked out to the road and stopped me, I was biking up our street. She gave me a kind wave and a grin.

"Hey, may I ride your bike?" she said.

I was taken aback. I thought, "Oh my god, I made a friend."

"Obviously," I said.

She climbed on and rode for about twenty or thirty feet while I got off. She stopped and got off as a random older child ran up to the street, and he got on and rode off. The fact that they had stolen my bicycle didn't really sink me since I was so thrilled that a female had talked to me. I skipped and grinned as I ran home. My cousin inquired about the location of the bicycle. I informed him.

He said, "You've been robbed, Trevor." "What prevented you from pursuing them?"

"I believed they were being kind. I believed I had made a buddy.

My guardian, Mlungisi, was older. After a half hour, he returned with my bike after running off to find the children.

Such incidents were frequent. I was constantly harassed. The worst of them was most likely the event at the mulberry tree. I was roaming around the neighborhood late one afternoon, playing alone as usual. Up the street, this group of five or six colored lads were gathering berries from the mulberry tree and consuming them. I went over and began selecting some for myself to take home. The boys were around twelve or thirteen years older than I was. I didn't speak to them, and neither did they speak to me. I could comprehend what they were saying because they were conversing in Afrikaans. Then one of them, this young man who was the group's ringleader, approached. "How do you moerbee, sien?" Are your mulberries visible to me? Once more, my initial thought was, "Oh, cool." I became friends. I showed him my mulberries by holding up my hand. Then he smashed them into the floor after knocking them out of my grasp. The other children burst out laughing. I stood there and gave him a quick glance. I had thickened my skin by then. Bullying was nothing new to me. I dismissed it and resumed my berry picking.

This boy began cursing me out, obviously not receiving the response he was looking for. Boesman, jou onnosele jou weg! "Leave this place immediately! Get out of here, you dumb Bushie! Bushman! I ignored him and carried on with my activities. A splash on the back of my skull followed. He would use a mulberry to strike me. It was shocking, but not unpleasant. He struck me in the face once again as I turned to face him.

Then all of these kids started throwing berries at me, pelting the living daylights out of me, before I could even respond. Some of the berries stung like pebbles and weren't ripe. I attempted to shield my face with my hands, but I was being bombarded from every direction. They were calling me derogatory names, laughing, and hurling objects at me. "Bushie! Bushman!" I was afraid. I wasn't sure what to do because of how abrupt it was. I began to cry and fled. All the way back down the road to our house, I fled for my life.

I was crying uncontrollably and drenched in reddish-purple berry juice as I dashed inside, looking as though I had been beaten to a pulp. My mom gave me a terrified look.

"What took place?"

I told her the story in between sobbing. "These kids threw berries at me from the mulberry tree." She started giggling as soon as I was done. "It's not amusing!" I exclaimed.

"No, Trevor," she responded. "I find it hilarious, but I'm not laughing. I'm giggling with relief. I believed you had been assaulted. I mistook this for blood. The fact that it's just berry juice makes me laugh.

My mother found it all amusing. She could tackle any topic with comedy, no matter how dark or terrible. She laughed and gestured to the half of me dripping dark berry juice, saying, "Look on the bright side." "You are actually half white and half black now."

"It's not amusing!"

"You're fine, Trevor," she said. "Go wash yourself up. You're not injured. Emotionally, you're hurt. However, you're unharmed.

Abel arrived half an hour later. Abel was still my mom's boyfriend at that time. Really, he wasn't attempting to be my father or even my stepfather. He resembled an older brother more than anything else. He would have fun and play about with me. Despite the fact that I didn't know him well, I was aware of his temper. Extremely hilarious and charming when he felt like it, but dammit he could also be cruel. He had been raised in the homelands, where survival was a struggle. Abel was also tall, perhaps six feet three, and slender. He hadn't yet struck my mother. Nor had he struck me yet. However, I was aware of his risk. I had witnessed it. In traffic, someone would cut us off. Out of the window, Abel would shout. The other man would respond with a shout and a honk. Abel would quickly leave our car and go to theirs, snatch the man through the driver's side window, yell in his face, and raise his fist. The other guy would go into a panic. "Whoa, whoa, whoa. I apologize, I apologize.

Abel noticed that I had been crying when he came in that evening and sat down on the couch.

"What took place?" he asked.

I began to describe. My mom interrupted me. "Avoid telling him," she advised. She was aware of what would occur. She was more knowledgeable than I was.

"What don't you tell me?" "Abel said."

"It isn't anything," she stated.

I answered, "It's not nothing."

She gave me a scowl. "Avoid telling him."

Abel was growing impatient. "What? Why don't you tell me?

He had been drinking; his temper always became worse after drinking, and he never returned home from work sober. It was odd, but I knew then that I could convince him to intervene and take action if I said the proper words. We were practically family, and I knew he would assist me in getting even with the boys if I made him feel as though his family had been wronged. I detested the fact that I knew he harbored a devil; his violent and deadly outbursts frightened me. However, I knew exactly what I needed to say to win the beast over to my cause at that very time.

I described the incident to him, including the names they used and the manner in which I was attacked. My mother kept laughing it off and telling me it was nothing to worry about because it was just kids being kids. I was unable to perceive that she was attempting to diffuse the issue. I was simply upset with her. It's not funny, even when you believe it to be a joke! It's not amusing!

Abel did not laugh. I could see his rage growing as I explained what the bullies had done to him. There was no screaming or clenching of fists when Abel was angry. Without a word, he sat on the couch and listened to me. Then, with great composure and purpose, he got up.

He said, "Take me to these boys."

This is it, I thought. My revenge will be exacted by my big brother.

We climbed into his vehicle and proceeded up the road, coming to a stop a short distance from the tree. With the exception of the streetlamps, it was now dark, yet we could still see the lads playing beneath the tree. I gestured toward the leader. "That one. He was the primary one. With a smack of his foot on the gas, Abel leaped into the grass and headed directly for the tree's base. He leaped out. I leaped out. The children knew exactly what was happening as soon as they saw me. They fled like crazy and dispersed.

Abel moved quickly. He was quick, for heaven's sake. The leader of the ring had fled and was attempting to scale a wall. Abel caught hold of him, hauled him back, and pulled him down. He then began beating him after removing a switch and a branch from the tree. I enjoyed it when he beat the living daylights out of him. That moment was the most enjoyable thing I have ever experienced. Revenge is really nice. Although it transports you to a dark place, it quenches your need, guy.

Then it flipped in the most bizarre time. When I saw the terrified expression on the boy's face, I knew that Abel had gone beyond retaliating against me. He had no intention of teaching the child a lesson. He was simply beating him. His anger was directed at a twelve-year-old youngster by a grown guy. I quickly swung from saying, "Yes, I got my revenge," to saying, "No, no, no." Too much. Too much. Oh no. Oh no. Oh no. What have I done, God?

Abel pulled this kid to the car and held him up in front of me after he had been beaten to shit. "Express regret." The child was trembling and sobbing. I had never seen terror in someone's eyes until he looked me in the eye. A stranger had beaten him in a manner that I doubt he had ever experienced before. He apologized, but it didn't seem like it was for what he had done to me. He seemed to be apologizing for all of his transgressions because he was unaware that such a punishment was possible.

I saw how much that boy and I had in common when I looked into his eyes. He was a child. I was a child. He was in tears. I was in tears. He learned to hate and to despise himself while growing up in South Africa as a colored boy. He needed to bully me because of who had bullied him? I unleashed my own horror on his world in retaliation for him making me feel afraid. However, I was aware that I had done something awful.

Abel kicked and pushed the child away after he apologized. "Go." We drove silently back to the house after the child ran off. Abel and my mother got into a heated argument at home. She often criticized him for losing his anger. "You cannot attack other people's kids all the time! The law does not apply to you! This rage isn't a way of life!

The father of this child came to our house a few hours later to confront Abel. I stayed inside the house and watched Abel go out to the gate. Abel was really inebriated by then. The father of this child had no idea what he was getting himself into. He was a middle-aged, mild-mannered man. I spent the entire time observing Abel, so I don't recall anything about him. I didn't look away from him. I was aware of the danger there.

Abel eventually acquired a gun, which he did not have at the time. However, Abel might instill fear of God in you without a gun. He got right in this guy's face, and I saw it. I heard Abel, but I couldn't hear what the other man was saying. "Avoid messing with me. I'll murder you. With a swift turn, the man returned to his vehicle and drove off. He believed he was come to protect his family's honor. He was glad to get away with his life.

Chapter 10: A Young Man's Long, Awkward, Occasionally Tragic, and Frequently Humiliating Education in Affairs of the Heart, Part I: Valentine's Day

I had just relocated from Maryvale to H. A. Jack, a primary school, and it was my first year there. Valentine's Day was drawing near rapidly. I had never celebrated Valentine's Day before, and I was twelve years old. It was not observed at the Catholic school. Valentine's Day made sense to me conceptually. You fall in love after the nude infant shoots you with an arrow. That part I understood. However, I had never heard of it as an activity before. Valentine's Day served as a fundraising event for H. A. Jack. I had to go ask a friend what was going on since students were selling cards and flowers.

"What is this?" "I said." "What are we doing?"
"Oh, it's Valentine's Day," she remarked. When you declare your love for a certain someone, they reciprocate your feelings.
That seems intense, I thought. However, Cupid's arrow had not struck me, and I was unaware of anyone who had been shot on my behalf. I didn't know what was happening. Throughout the week, the schoolgirls would ask, "Who is your Valentine? Who is your special someone? I had no idea what I was meant to do. Eventually, a white girl responded, "You ought to ask Maylene." The other children concurred. Indeed, Maylene. You ought to consult Maylene, for sure. You must speak with Maylene. You two are meant to be together.

I used to walk home from school with a girl named Maylene. Now, my mom, my stepfather Abel, my new baby brother Andrew, and I all lived in the city. In order to finance Abel's new garage, we had to sell our Eden Park home. After that, things fell apart, and we moved to Highlands North, which is a half-hour walk from H. A. Jack. Every afternoon, a bunch of us would leave school together, with each child splitting off and heading off to their own home. We would always be the final two because Maylene and I lived the furthest away. After walking together till we reached our destination, we would split off.

Maylene was calm. She was clever, pretty, and an excellent tennis player. She was someone I liked. I wasn't really considering ladies in that sense yet, therefore I didn't have a crush on her. I simply enjoyed spending time with her. In addition, Maylene was the only girl of color at school. At school, I was the only mixed child. The only two individuals that shared a similar appearance were us. When I asked Maylene to be my Valentine, the white girls insisted.
"Trevor, you need to ask her," they said. There are only two of you. You are accountable for it. It seemed as though if we didn't mate and continue, our species would become extinct. which, as I've discovered in my life, white folks do without even recognizing it. "We have to set you up for sex because you two look alike."
When the girls brought it up, I honestly hadn't considered asking Maylene, but when someone implants an idea in your mind, it alters your perspective.

"Maylene has a serious crush on you."
"Does she?"
"Yes, you two get along really well!"
"Are we?"
"Yes, absolutely."
"All right. if you say so.
I guess I liked Maylene as much as I liked anyone. For the most part, I believe I enjoyed the thought of being appreciated. I made the decision to ask her to be my Valentine, but I was clueless on how to go about it. I had absolutely no idea what a girlfriend was. The entire school administration had to be explained to me. There was the situation where you don't speak directly to the person. She has her own group of friends, and you have yours. Your group of friends must approach her group of friends and inform them that Trevor has feelings for Maylene. He desires her as his Valentine's Day gift. We support it. With your permission, we can now sign off. "All right," her

companions remark. It sounds good. We must have Maylene run it. They visit Maylene. They confer. They express their opinions to her. According to Trevor, he likes you. We support it. We believe that you two would get along well. What are your thoughts? I like Trevor, Maylene says. "All right," they say. Let's proceed. They return to us. "Maylene says she's waiting for Trevor's Valentine's Day advance and she approves."

The females informed me that this procedure was necessary. "Cool," I said. Let's get it done. Maylene agreed, the pals worked things out, and I was set.

I was attempting to summon the guts to ask Maylene as we walked home together the week before Valentine's Day. I felt really anxious. It was unlike anything I had ever done. Her buddies had informed me that she would say yes, so I already knew the answer. It is comparable to serving in Congress. Even though you are aware of the votes before you take the floor, it is still challenging since anything can happen. I waited until we were outside McDonald's because I had no idea how to do it and I just wanted it to be flawless. After that, I mustered up the confidence to face her.

"Hey, would you be my Valentine's Day partner? Valentine's Day is approaching."
Indeed. Your Valentine will be me.

We then shared a kiss beneath the golden arches. I had never kissed a girl before. Even though it was only a quick kiss and our lips only made contact for a few seconds, it caused my mind to explode. Indeed! Yes, indeed. This. I like this, but I have no idea what it is. Someone had woken up. It was particularly memorable because it was directly outside McDonald's.

I was genuinely thrilled now. I had a Valentine's Day card. I was in a relationship. I wanted to make Maylene's Valentine's Day as special as possible, so I thought about her all week. I bought her a card, a teddy bear, and flowers with the pocket money I had saved up. Since there aren't many nice phrases that rhyme with Maylene, it was incredibly difficult for me to write a poem with her name on the card. (Machine? A ravine? Sardine? Then the moment arrived. I prepared my Valentine's Day card, flowers, and teddy bear and brought them to school. I was the world's happiest boy.

Before recess, the teachers had scheduled a time for everyone to exchange Valentines. I knew Maylene would be in the corridor outside our classes, so I waited for her there. Love blossomed all around me. Boys and girls sharing gifts and cards, giggling, and kissing each other. I kept on waiting. Maylene finally arrived and approached me. I started to say "Happy Valentine's Day!" when she interrupted me, saying, "Oh, hello, Trevor." Listen, I am no longer able to be your girlfriend. I am now Lorenzo's girlfriend and not yours because he requested me to be his Valentine's Day present and I am unable to have two Valentines.

I didn't know how to take it in because she stated it so casually. Since I had never had a girlfriend before, I initially assumed that this was just the way things work.

"Oh, all right," I replied. "Well, happy Valentine's Day, I guess."

I displayed the teddy bear, the card, and the flowers. She accepted them, thanked them, and left.

I had the impression that someone had fired holes in every portion of me with a gun. However, a part of me simultaneously thought, "Well, this makes sense." Everything I wasn't, Lorenzo was. He was well-liked. He was Caucasian. He would ask out the school's lone colored female, upsetting the delicate balance. He was as stupid as rocks, but girls adored him. Kind of a bad boy, yet a nice man. He was that guy who had girls do his schoolwork. He was also really attractive. It seemed as though he exchanged all of his intelligence points for beauty points as he was developing his character. I had no chance.

Even though I was devastated, I could understand Maylene's decision. I also would have chosen Lorenzo above myself. I returned to the classroom, sat alone, and waited for the bell to sound while the other children ran up and down the hallways and out on the playground, laughing and smiling with their red and pink cards and flowers.

Chapter 11: Outsider

I enrolled in Sandringham High School's grade eight after completing my elementary education at H. A. Jack. Even after apartheid ended, the majority of Black people continued to reside in townships and the erstwhile homeland areas, where the only government schools were the dilapidated Bantu system. Rich white children were hiding away in private schools, which were extremely costly but almost always assured admission to universities, together with the few black, colored, and Indian children who had money or could receive scholarships. Sandringham was classified as a Model C school, which means it was a hybrid of private and public education, much like American charter schools. There were a thousand children on the expansive grounds, which included a swimming pool, sports fields, and tennis courts.

There are no cafeterias in South African schools. At Sandringham, we would purchase our lunch at what we refer to as the "tuck shop," a little canteen, and then be allowed to eat anywhere on the school grounds, including the playground, the courtyard, and the quad. Children would separate and form groups and cliques. You could see how people merged and darkened into one another, even though most people were still grouped by color. The majority of the children playing soccer were Black. The majority of the children playing tennis were white. The children that participated in cricket were diverse. Beside the prefabricated buildings, the Chinese children would congregate. On the quad, the matrics, or seniors as they are known in South Africa, would congregate. Computer gurus would congregate over there, and popular, attractive girls would congregate here. Race overlapped class and location in the actual world, which is why the categories were racial to the extent that they were. Children from the suburbs congregated with one another. Township children socialized with one another.

I encountered the similar situation in the playground at H. A. during break, where I was the only mixed child among a thousand. Jack: Where should I have gone? I didn't naturally belong to any one of the numerous organizations that were available to me. I was clearly not

Chinese or Indian. I was constantly spat on by the colored kids because I was too black. I was therefore not welcome there. The white kids were always going shopping, going to the movies, and taking trips—things that required money—but I was good enough with them, as usual, to avoid being tormented. I wasn't included there either because we didn't have any money. The impoverished black children were the group I identified with the most. Although I got along with them and spent time with them, the majority of them traveled to school in minibuses from Soweto, Tembisa, and Alexandra, which were located far out in the townships. They rode together to school and returned home together. They were divided into groups. They were spending time together on the weekends and throughout school breaks, and I was unable to go. It took me forty minutes to drive from my place to Soweto. We were short on cash for gas. I was alone after school. I was alone on the weekends. Always the outsider, I made up my own bizarre little universe. I had no choice but to do it. I needed to blend in somehow. In order to purchase the same snacks and engage in the activities that the other children were doing, I also needed money. That's how I ended up being the tuck-shop guy.

Every day I was late since I had a lengthy walk to school. To write my name down for detention, I would need to make a brief stop in the prefect's office. The patroness of detention was me. I would rush to my morning classes, whether they were in biology, English, or algebra, even though I was already late. Assembly was the final period before the break. The professors and prefects would go up onstage and discuss the school's activities, including announcements, prizes, and other things, while the students gathered in the assembly hall, sat row by row by grade. At every assembly, the names of the children in jail were announced, and I was always one of them. Always. Each and every day. The joke was a running one. "Detentions for today," the prefect would say, and I would instantly get up. I was Meryl Streep, and it was similar to the Oscars. On one occasion, I got up, and the prefect announced the five individuals, but I wasn't one of them. Everyone started giggling. Someone shouted, "Where is Trevor?!" The prefect shook his head after taking a look at the article. "Nope." The hall exploded in applause and cheers. "Hooray!"

The line to purchase food was so long that there would be a rush to the tuck shop right after assembly. Your break time was being deducted for each minute you were in line. You had more time to eat, play soccer, or just hang out if you received your food sooner. Additionally, the greatest meal was gone if you arrived late.

At that age, I was true to two things. First of all, I was still the school's fastest student. Secondly, I lacked pride. I would dash to the tuck shop as soon as we were freed from assembly so that I could be the first one there. I was in line first all the time. People started lining up to me because I was so well-known for being that man. "Hey, could you get me this?" which, since it was essentially cutting the line, would annoy the youngsters behind me. At assembly, people began to approach me. "Hey, I have ten rand," they would say. I'll give you two if you buy me some food. I discovered then that time is money. I came to the realization that since I was willing to run for it, people would pay me to buy their meal. At assembly, I began to say, "Place your orders. I'll purchase your food if you give me a list of your preferences and a portion of your budget.

I became successful overnight. My best customers were fat males. They couldn't run, but they loved to eat. I had all these white, obese, wealthy kids who said, "This is amazing! I have money, my parents treat me, and now I have a method to acquire meals without working for it—and I still get my break. I was turning away children because I had so many customers. I had a rule: only high bidders may place five orders every day. I would earn so much that I could use the money from other children to buy my lunch and keep the money my mother gave me for pocket money. After that, I could save money for anything I wanted or take the bus home rather than walking. After assembly was finished each day, I would make a hurried dash to get everyone's hot dogs, Cokes, and muffins. You could even let me know where you'd be and I'd deliver it to you if you paid me more.

I had discovered my specialty. I developed the ability to switch between groups with ease because I didn't belong to any. I was able to float. I was a cultural chameleon, and I still am. I became proficient at blending. I could join the jocks in sports. I could converse with the nerds about computers. I could join the township youngsters in dancing and jumping in the circle. I visited everyone while working, chatting, making deliveries, and cracking jokes.

I was like a food dealer for marijuana. At the gathering, the cannabis guy is always welcome. Although he is not a member of the circle, his contributions have led to his temporary inclusion. I was that person. A stranger at all times. You can hide behind a shell, remain anonymous, and be invisible as the outsider. You can also go the opposite route. You open up to protect yourself. You just ask to be accepted for the one aspect of yourself that you are prepared to share, not for acceptance of who you are in your entirety. It was funny to me. I discovered that I could be a part of any group that was laughing, while not being a member of any particular group. I would stop by, distribute the goodies, and crack a few jokes. I would entertain them. I would listen to a little of what they were saying, find out more about their group, and then go. I never remained longer than was necessary. I wasn't an outcast, but I wasn't popular either. In addition to being everywhere with everyone, I was also alone.

Chapter 12: A Young Man's Long, Awkward, Occasionally Tragic, and Frequently Humiliating Education in Affairs of the Heart, Part II: The Crush

I was not afflicted with the attention of girls in high school. In class, I wasn't the most attractive guy. In class, I wasn't even the cool guy. I was unattractive. I had a rough time with puberty. People used to wonder what was wrong with me because my acne was so awful, as if I had experienced an allergic response. It was the type of acne that is considered a disease. "Acne vulgaris," the physician said. Children, we're not discussing pimples. The term "pustules" refers to large, pus-filled blackheads and whiteheads. They tore through my entire face, beginning on my forehead and moving down the sides, covering my cheeks and neck.

It didn't help that I was poor. I had a large, messy Afro because I couldn't afford a good haircut. In addition, my mother used to get upset when I outgrew my school uniforms too quickly, so she started purchasing me clothes that were three sizes too big in order to save money. My shoes flopped, my slacks were too loose, and my blazer was too long. I was a clown. According to Murphy's Law, I stopped growing the year my mother started purchasing me clothing that were too big. I was therefore stuck as a clown and would never be able to grow out of my clown attire. The only positive thing about me was my height, but even that made me look gangly and ungainly. Duck feet. High ass. Nothing was successful.

I gained important dating knowledge after being heartbroken on Valentine's Day by Maylene and the attractive, pleasant Lorenzo. I discovered that funny guys get to hang out with the cool guys and their girlfriends, and cool guys get chicks. I didn't have any girlfriends since I wasn't a cool man. I soon grasped that formula and recognized where I belonged. I never asked any girls out. There was no girlfriend for me. I made no attempt at all.

The natural order of things would have been upset if I had tried to get a girl. Because I was nobody, I was accepted everywhere, which contributed to my career as the tuck-shop guy. I was the clown with duck feet and floppy shoes who had pimples. The boys didn't see me as a threat. The girls didn't see me as a threat. I ran the risk of no longer being accepted as nobody the moment I became famous. The attractive girls were already taken. The well-liked men had made their claim. You knew that if you did anything with Zuleika, there would be a fight because they would say, "I like Zuleika." It was wise to keep out of danger and on the periphery in order to survive.

The only time I got attention from the females at Sandringham was when they asked me to deliver a letter to the class's attractive guy. However, there was a girl named Johanna who I knew. Throughout our lives, Johanna and I had attended the same school on and off. Together, we attended Maryvale for preschool. She then proceeded to another school after leaving. Then, we attended H. A. Jack together for elementary school. She then proceeded to another school after leaving. At last, we found ourselves together at Sandringham. We became buddies as a result.

Among the popular girls was Johanna. Zaheera was her best buddy. Johanna was stunning. Zaheera looked beautiful. Cape Malay, Zaheera was colored. She reminded me of Salma Hayek. The males were all attracted to Johanna since she was out and about kissing them. There weren't as many guys after Zaheera because, despite her beauty, she was incredibly shy.

Zaheera and Johanna were never apart. They were three grades above me in popularity, yet they were one grade below me. Nevertheless, because I knew Johanna and we had a connection from attending separate schools, I was able to spend time with them. Although I couldn't date girls, I could make them laugh, so I was still able to chat to them. People enjoy laughing, and I'm fortunate that attractive girls are also people. In that sense, I could identify with them, but not the other way around. I was aware of this as they would ask, "So how do you think I can get Daniel to ask me out?" after they had stopped laughing at my stories and jokes. I always knew exactly where I stood.

I had worked hard to project an image of myself as the humorous, unthreatening guy, but in reality, I was completely smitten with Zaheera. She was hilarious and very attractive. We would get together and talk a lot. I couldn't stop thinking about her, but I never thought I was good enough to date her. I convinced myself that I would only ever have a crush on her for the rest of my life.

I eventually made the decision to lay out a plan. I made the decision to be best friends with Zaheera and to stick with her long enough to invite her to our senior prom, also known as the matric dance. Keep in mind that we were now in grade nine. Three years had passed since the matric dance. However, I made the long-term decision. "Yeah," I said, "just going to take my time." Because, you know, that's what happens in the movies. I had watched my high school films in America. You stay around long enough for the girl to date a number of attractive jerks while the amiable good guy dates you, and then one day she turns around and says, "Oh, it's you." You were always the one. All along, you were the man I was meant to be with.

That was my strategy. It was infallible.

I spent as much time as possible with Zaheera. We would discuss the boys, who liked her, and which ones liked her. I would advise her. She was matched up with this guy named Gary at one time. They began dating. In a sort of arranged marriage, Gary and Zaheera were paired together by their friends since Gary was in the popular group but somewhat shy, and Zaheera was also in the popular group but somewhat shy. However, Zaheera had no fondness for Gary. She informed me. We discussed everything.

I don't know how, but one day I worked up the nerve to ask Zaheera for her phone number. This was significant at the time since, unlike now, when everyone has their number for messaging and other purposes, it wasn't a mobile number. The landline was this. to her home. where her parents may respond. One afternoon at school, we were chatting when I said, "Could I have your phone number? Perhaps I could give you a call and we could have a conversation at home. When she said "yes," my head blew up. What? I'm getting a girl's phone number? This is crazy! What should I do? I felt really anxious. She told me the numbers one by one while I was writing them down and attempting to keep my hand from shaking, and I will never forget that. I said, "All right, Trevor," as we said our goodbyes and parted ways to class. Keep your cool. Do not give her a call immediately. That evening, I gave her a call. seven o'clock. At two, she had given me her number. I was being cool there. Don't call her at five o'clock, dude. It's too clear. Give her a call at seven o'clock.

I called her home that evening. Her mother replied. "Please let me talk to Zaheera," I pleaded. She answered the phone when her mother called, and we spoke. For about an hour. Following that, we began speaking more on the phone and in school. I never expressed my feelings to her. Never moved. Nothing. I was too afraid all the time.

Gary and Zaheera split up. After that, they reconciled. Then they split up. After that, they reconciled. She didn't like their first kiss, so they never shared another one. Then they actually broke up. I waited through everything. I was still the nice friend even after I saw Popular Gary burn to the ground. Yes, the strategy is effective. Here comes the matric dance. Just two and a half years remain…

The mid-year school holidays followed. Zaheera was absent from school on the day we returned. The following day, she did not attend school. The following day, she did not attend school. After a while, I went to find Johanna on the quad.

"Where is Zaheera?" "I said." She has been absent for some time. Is she ill?

"No," she replied. "Has nobody informed you? She walked out of the school. She no longer visits this place.

"What?"

"Yes, she did go."

My initial reaction was, "Wow, all right." That is noteworthy. To catch up, I should phone her.

I inquired, "What school did she transfer to?"

"She didn't. In America, her father found employment. They relocated there during the interval. They have left the country.

"What?"

Indeed. She is no longer there. She was also a wonderful friend. I'm quite depressed. Do you feel as depressed as I do?

I answered, still trying to take it all in, "Uh...yeah." "I enjoyed Zaheera." She was very awesome.

Yes, she had a major crush on you, which is why she was also really depressed. She waited for you to ask her out all the time. Alright, I have to leave for class! Goodbye!

I stood there in disbelief as she fled. She had suddenly thrown me a lot of information, first that Zaheera was gone, then that she had departed for America, and last that she had always liked me. I felt as though I had been struck by three waves of heartbreak, each more intense than the one before. I thought about all the times I could have said, "Hey, Zaheera, I like you," and all the hours we had spent on the phone and on the quad. Are you going to be my girlfriend? If I had the guts to utter them, these ten words could have altered my life. However, I hadn't, and she had now left.

Chapter 13: Colorblind

Teddy was the only child I got to know at Sandringham. Funny man, really endearing. He had a mischievous smile with two large teeth that protruded from the front of his mouth, and my mother used to call him Bugs Bunny. One of those buddies you start hanging out with and never see again, Teddy and I got along like a house on fire. Additionally, we were both naughty as crap. I had at last found someone who made me feel normal in Teddy. I was the family's dread. He was his family's dread. It was chaos when you placed us together. We would toss pebbles through windows on our way home from school, only to watch them break, and then flee. We were always in custody together. Everyone in the school, including the principal, professors, and students, knew that Teddy and Trevor were best friends.

Teddy's mother was employed by a family in Linksfield, a posh suburb close to the school, as a domestic worker. Although it took almost forty minutes to walk from my place to Linksfield, it was still feasible. In any case, I spent much of my time walking about back then. There was nothing else I could do, and there was no other way I could afford to go. You were my friend if you enjoyed going for walks. Together, Teddy and I strolled about Johannesburg. Teddy and I would hang out at his house after I walked there. After that, we would stroll back to my place and spend time there. To hang out, we would walk the three hours or so from my place to the city center, and then we would walk back.

On Fridays and Saturdays, we would stroll to the shopping center and spend time together. My house was only a few blocks from the Balfour Park Shopping Mall. Although it's not a large mall, it has everything: eateries, a movie theater, an arcade, and South Africa's equivalent of Target and the Gap. When we arrived at the mall, we would simply stroll around because we never had any money to shop, see movies, or buy meals.

When we visited the mall one evening, the most of the stores were closed, but the theater was still operating, thus the structure was still open. A metal gate, resembling a trellis, was dragged across the entry and padlocked when the stationery store that sold magazines and greeting cards closed at night because it lacked a door. Teddy and I were walking past this store when we noticed that we could reach the chocolate rack inside by sticking our arms through the trellis. Furthermore, these chocolates weren't just any chocolates; they contained booze. I was a huge drinker. I adored it. I've always taken sips of adults' drinks whenever I could.

After grabbing several, we drank the whiskey inside and devoured the chocolates. We'd struck gold. We began returning time and time again to steal more. After waiting for the stores to begin closing, we would go sit against the gate and pretend that we were just chatting. After making sure everything was in order, one of us would reach in, take a chocolate, and sip the whiskey. Grab a chocolate, reach in, and sip the rum. Grab a chocolate and sip on the brandy. We had a great time doing this every weekend for at least a month. Then we overplayed our hand.

The night was a Saturday. We were lingering at the stationery storefront, leaning against the gate. Just as I reached in to grab a chocolate, a mall cop rounded the corner and seen me with my arm up to my shoulder. I held out my hand, containing some chocolates. It resembled a movie almost exactly. I caught a glimpse of him. He noticed me. His eyes widened. I made an effort to leave, behaving normally. Then he exclaimed, "Hey! Stop!

The pursuit was underway. We ran and made our way to the entrance. We were hauling ass as quickly as we could since I knew we would be imprisoned if a guard stopped us at the exit. We got out. At least a dozen mall police officers were pursuing us from all sides as soon as we pulled into the parking lot. I had my head down as I ran. I was known to these guards. I spent all of my time in that mall. My mother was also known to the guards. That mall was where she conducted her banking. I would have been dead if they had even seen me.

With the guards shouting directly behind us, we dashed across the parking lot, dodging and swerving between parked cars. After reaching the gas station, we dashed through it and turned left into the main road. It was amazing as they chased and chased and we fled and ran. Being wicked was half the fun, and now the hunt was on. The chance of being caught was the other half. I really enjoyed it. I loved it even though I was fecesing myself. It was my territory. I lived in this neighborhood. You couldn't find me in my community. I was familiar with every street and alley, every rear wall to scale, and every fence with a gap large enough to squeeze through. I was familiar with every possible shortcut. I was constantly planning my escape as a child, no matter where I went or what building I was in. Just in case something went wrong. In my imagination, I was a significant and dangerous man who needed to know the locations of all the cameras and the exits, but in reality, I was a nerdy child with virtually no friends.

We couldn't run indefinitely, I knew. We required a strategy. There was a road to the left that led to a dead end and a metal gate as Teddy and I passed the fire station. I was aware that there was a gap in the fence that I could squeeze through, and that there was an empty field on the other side, beyond the shopping center, which led back to the main road and my house. A child could squeeze through the opening, but an adult couldn't. My years of fantasizing about being a covert agent have finally paid off. I had an escape now that I needed one.

"This way, Teddy!" I shouted.

It's a dead end, I say!

"We can succeed! Come with me!

He didn't. After turning, I came to a dead end. Teddy broke in the opposite direction. He was followed by half of the mall cops and I by the other half. When I reached the barrier, I knew just how to wriggle under it. One leg, then the other, then the head, then the shoulder—done. I was done. The guards were unable to follow me once they struck the barrier behind me. Three blocks from my house, I was on the road after running across the field to a fence on the far side and popping through. I put my hands in my pockets and strolled home, just another innocuous person taking a walk.

I waited for Teddy when I returned home. He failed to appear. I waited for thirty, forty, and an hour. Teddy, no.

Fuck.

I sprinted to Linksfield to visit Teddy. Teddy, no. The morning of Monday, I went to school. Teddy is still absent.

Fuck.

I was now concerned. I went home after school and looked again, but there was nothing there. Nothing at Teddy's house again. I then sprinted home.

Teddy's parents arrived an hour later. At the door, my mother greeted them.

They said, "Teddy was arrested for shoplifting."

Fuuuck.

From the next room, I overheard their entire exchange. My mother was convinced I was engaged from the beginning.

She said, "Well, where was Trevor?"

They said, "Teddy claimed he wasn't with Trevor."

My mother wasn't convinced. "Well. Do you really think Trevor wasn't involved?

No, it seems not. According to the police, there was another child, but he escaped.

"It was Trevor, then."

"No, Teddy told us it wasn't Trevor when we asked him. It was another child, he claimed.

"Oh, all right." I was summoned in by my mother. "Are you aware of this matter?"

"What is it?"

"Teddy was caught stealing from a store."

"What?" I pretended to be stupid. "Nope. That is absurd. It's unbelievable. Teddy? No.

What happened to you?" my mother inquired.

"I was in my house."

"But Teddy is with you all the time."

I gave a shrug. "Well, I guess not this time."

My mother briefly believed she had caught me red-handed, but Teddy had provided me with a strong alibi. I returned to my room, believing that I was safe.

My name was called over the PA system the following day while I was in class. "Trevor Noah, please come to the office of the principal." Every child exclaimed, "Ooooohhh." The entire school now knew I was in trouble because the announcements could be heard in every classroom. I rose and made my way to the office, where I waited nervously on a wooden seat outside the door.

At last, Mr. Friedman, the principal, left. "Come in, Trevor." The chief of mall security, two uniformed police officers, and Mrs. Vorster, Teddy's and my homeroom teacher, were waiting inside his office. Above me, the guilty young black man, stood a room full of quiet, stony-faced white authority figures. I had a racing heart. I sat down.

Mr. Friedman remarked, "Trevor, I don't know if you know this, but Teddy was arrested the other day."

"What?" I went through the entire process again. Teddy? Oh, no. For what purpose?

For stealing from stores. He has been expelled and will not be returning to school. These officers are visiting local schools to look into the matter because we know there was another boy involved. Mrs. Vorster told us that you were Teddy's best friend, so we called you here to ask whether you knew anything about it.

I gave a headshake. "No, I have no knowledge."

"Are you aware of Teddy's companion?"

"No."

"All right." He got up and went to the television in the room's corner. "The entire incident is captured on camera by the cops, Trevor. We would like you to look at it.

Fuuuu-uuuuu-uuck.

My chest was thumping with my heart. Life has been enjoyable, I thought. I'm going to be dismissed. I will be incarcerated. It's this.

Mr. Friedman hit the VCR's Play button. The tape began. Despite the poor, black-and-white security camera film, it was easy to see what was going on. Teddy and I reached through the gate, and they even had it from several perspectives. Teddy and I hurried to the door. The entire thing was theirs. A few seconds later, Mr. Friedman reached up and, from a few meters away, freeze-framed it in the center of the screen, pausing it with me. I imagined that he would turn to face me at this point and ask, "Are you ready to confess now?" He didn't.

"Do you know of any white kids that Teddy hangs out with, Trevor?" he said.

I almost broke myself. "What?"

Teddy was dark, I realized as I glanced at the screen. I have olive skin and am light. However, the camera is unable to simultaneously expose for light and dark. Therefore, the camera is unsure of what to do when I am placed next to a black person on a black-and-white screen. The camera selects me as white if it must. It blows out my color. There was a white person and a black person in this video. Nevertheless, it was me. Despite the poor quality of the photo and the somewhat hazy facial characteristics, it was me if you looked closely. Teddy's best friend was me. Teddy just had me as a friend. The most likely accomplice was myself alone. At the very least, you had to suspect me. They didn't. They were so certain that I had to know who this white child was that they interrogated me for a full ten minutes.

Teddy's best friend is you, Trevor. Be honest with us. Who is this child?

"I'm not sure."

"You don't even recognize him?"

"No."

"You never heard of him from Teddy?"

"Never."

After a while, Mrs. Vorster simply began listing all the white children she believed it may be.

"Is David here?"

"No."

"Rian?"

"No."

"Frederik?"

"No."

I kept expecting them to turn around and shout, "It's you!" as if it were a trick. They didn't. I felt so invisible at one point that I nearly wanted to claim the credit. I wanted to leap up and yell, "Are you people blind?," while pointing at the TV. That's who I am! Is it not obvious to you that that is me? Naturally, though, I didn't. And they were unable to. The white guy they were looking for was sitting directly in front of them, but these people were too blinded by their own racial construct to notice it.

I was eventually sent back to class. I waited for my mom to receive the call for the remainder of the day and the following few weeks, hoping that the other shoe would drop. "He's with us! We worked it out! However, the call never arrived.

Chapter 14: A Young Man's Long, Awkward, Occasionally Tragic, and Frequently Humiliating Education in Affairs of the Heart, Part III: The Dance

I would be a mogul by the time I graduated from high school. Selling unlicensed CDs that I created at home was part of my mini-empire that had grown out of my tuck-shop company. Even though she was frugal, I had persuaded my mother that I needed a computer for school. I didn't. I wanted it so I could play Leisure Suit Larry and browse the Internet. She caved down and got it for me, though, because I was so persuasive. I was in business because of the computer, the Internet, and the lucky CD writer that a buddy gave me.

I had found my specialty and was enjoying myself so much that I didn't even consider dating as an outsider. My computer's nude chicks were the only girls I ever knew. Occasionally, I would experiment with porn websites while downloading music and playing around in chat rooms. Pictures alone, of course, no video. With dial-up, it took a long time for the images to load, but with online porn these days, you just dive right in. Compared to now, it was almost gentlemanly. You would come to know her as a person by spending at least five minutes examining her face. You would then get some boobs a few minutes later. You had spent a great deal of time together by the time you reached her vagina.

The grade twelve matric dance was approaching in September. Senior prom. The big one was this. Valentine's Day presented me with yet another perplexing custom that I did not comprehend. All I knew about prom was that it's where it happens, based on my American movies. Your virginity is lost. Before you and the girl do the thing, you go and take a ride in the limousine. I literally just had that as a reference. However, I was aware of the rule: Funny guys get to hang out with the cool guys and their girlfriends, and cool guys get chicks. Therefore, I had anticipated that I would either not go or that I would not go with a date if I did.

In my CD company, I had two intermediaries, Bongani and Tom. In return for a portion, they sold the CDs that I had cloned. Tom and I met at the Balfour Park mall's arcade. His mother worked as a domestic servant, so he lived close by, much like Teddy. Although he attended Northview, a legitimate ghetto government school, Tom was in my grade. Over there, Tom was in charge of my CD sales.

Tom was a lively, talkative, and always on the go. He was also a true hustler who was constantly looking to work an angle or close a deal. He was able to persuade others to do anything. He is a wonderful man, but he is also completely dishonest and insane. On one occasion, I accompanied him to Hammanskraal, a settlement that resembled a homeland but wasn't. As the Afrikaans name implies, Hammanskraal was the kraal of Hamman, a farm that was once owned by a white man. The government established a barrier around the proper homelands, Venda, Gazankulu, and Transkei, where Black people genuinely resided, and told them to "stay there." On the map, Hammanskraal and similar communities were empty spaces where black people who had been deported had been resettled. The administration did just that. In order to provide four thousand homes with latrines, they would dig a series of trenches in a patch of dry, dusty, and unusable soil. After that, they would forcibly remove those who were inhabiting a white area illegally and abandon them in the middle of nowhere with several pallets of corrugated iron and plywood. "This is it. Your new home is here. Construct a few homes. Best of luck. We would see it on the news. It resembled a cold, survival-based reality TV show, except that no one made any money.

Tom informed me that we would be attending a talent event in Hammanskraal one day. I had purchased a pair of Timberland boots at the time. I had no other good clothes save for them. Timberlands were practically nonexistent in South Africa at the time. Because American rappers wore them, everyone desired them even though they were tough to obtain. To purchase them, I had scrambled and saved my CD money and tuck-shop money. "Make sure to wear your Timberlands," Tom said to me as we were heading out.

The talent event took place in this little, remote town hall that was tied to nothing. Tom was mingling with everyone and shaking hands when we arrived. There was poetry, dancing, and singing. The host then added, "Re na le modiragatsi yo o kgethegileng," as she stood up onstage. Ka kopo amogelang... "Spliff Star!" We have a unique performer who is a rapper from the United States. Welcome, please. "Spliff Star!"

At the time, Busta Rhymes' hype guy was Spliff Star. Bewildered, I sat there. What? Spliff Star? In the Hammanskraal? After that, everyone in the room turned to face me. Tom approached me and spoke softly into my ear.

"Come onstage, dude."

"What?"

"Enter the stage."

"What are you talking about, dude?"

"Dude, please, you're going to get me into a lot of trouble." I've already received payment from them.

"Cash? How much money?

Naturally, Tom had not informed me that he had informed these individuals that he would be bringing a well-known American rapper to perform in their talent event. I was that well-known American rapper in my Timberlands, and he had insisted on receiving payment in advance for doing so.

"Screw you," I called out. "I won't be leaving."

"Dude, I implore you, please. Do me a favor, please. Please. I told this girl that I knew all these rappers and that I wanted to date her. Please. I beseech you.

I'm not Spliff Star, dude. What should I do?

"Just rap songs by Busta Rhymes."

"However, none of the lyrics are familiar to me."

"It is irrelevant. English is not spoken by these folks.

"Fuck, aw."

I stumbled through some Busta Rhymes lyrics that I made up as I went along, while Tom performed some awful beat-boxing, "Bff ba-dff, bff bff ba-dff." Cheers and applause broke out from the audience. They had never witnessed anything so spectacular as the arrival of an American rapper in Hammanskraal.

That's Tom, then.

Tom stopped at my place one afternoon, and we immediately began discussing the dance. I informed him that I had no date, couldn't obtain one, and would never get one.

He offered to get a girl to accompany him to the dance.

"You can't," I said.

"I can, indeed. Let's come to an agreement.

"Tom, I'm not interested in any of your deals."

"Listen, here's the thing. I will return with the most gorgeous girl you have ever seen, and she will be your date to the dance, if you give me a larger share on the CDs I sell and a ton of free music for myself.

"All right, since that deal will never come up, I'll accept it."

"Is there a deal?"

"We have an agreement, but it will not be fulfilled."

"But is there a deal?"

"It's an agreement."

"All right, I'll get you a date. You will be a superstar when you take her to the matric dance because she will be the most gorgeous girl you have ever seen.

Two months remained till the dance. I quickly forgot about Tom and his absurd arrangement. Then one time he dropped by my place and peeked into my room.

"I located the girl."

"Really?"

Indeed. You must visit and get to know her.

I knew Tom was a jerk, but the hallmark of a great scammer is that they never give you anything in return. He gives you just enough to keep you on board. Tom had shown me a lot of attractive women. He was constantly with them and had a good game, but he was never dating them. I didn't question him when he claimed to have a girl. We boarded a bus together and went into the city.

The girl resided in a dilapidated apartment complex in the heart of the city. When we located her building, a girl waved us inside while leaning over the balcony. According to Tom, that was Lerato, the girl's sister. Tom was obviously working an angle since it turned out that he had been attempting to get with Lerato and that he had set me up with the sister as a means of getting in.

In the lobby, it was dark. We had to climb up several stories because the elevator was broken. Lerato took us into the apartment with this girl. This giant—I mean, this big, enormous woman—was in the living room.

I thought, "Oh, Tom." I see your actions here. Well done. Tom was also a great joker.

"Am I going on a date?" I inquired.

He responded, "No, no, no." "This date isn't for you. Her older sister is this one. Babiki is your date. Lerato is Babiki's younger sister; she has three older sisters. Babiki has gone to get groceries at the store. She will return shortly.

We talked to the older sister as we waited. After ten minutes, the door opened and the most stunning girl I've ever seen entered. Good Lord, she was. Gorgeous eyes and gorgeous golden-brown skin. She seemed to shine. She was unlike any girl at my high school.

"Hello," she said.

"Hello," I answered.

I was astounded. I didn't know how to approach such a stunning girl. She also didn't talk much because she was shy. The pause was a little awkward. Fortunately, Tom is an extremely talkative guy. Without hesitation, he went in and made everything easy. "This is Babiki, Trevor. Trevor, Babiki. He talked endlessly about how wonderful I was, how excited she was for the dance, when I would pick her up for it, and all the other specifics. After hanging out for a while, we left because Tom had to get somewhere. As we walked away, Babiki turned to wave and smile at me.

"Goodbye."

"Goodbye."

I was the happiest man alive as we left that place. It was unbelievable to me. At school, I was the guy who was unable to get a date. Since I didn't think I was worthy of a date, I had come to terms with the fact that I would never have one. Now, however, I was going to the matric dance with the world's most beautiful girl.

We visited Hillbrow a few more times in the ensuing weeks to spend time with Babiki, her sisters, and her friends. One of the lesser tribes in South Africa, the Pedi, was Babiki's family. It was enjoyable for me to meet folks from all backgrounds. We refer to Babiki and her companions as amabhujua. They attempt to pretend that they are not as impoverished as the majority of Black people. They appear wealthy and dress stylishly.

Amabhujua will place one shirt on layaway and pay it off over the course of seven months. They will wear thousands of dollars' worth of Italian leather shoes while living in shacks. A fascinating group of people.

I never went on a date with Babiki by myself. In a group, it was always just the two of us. We had a good time despite the fact that I was usually a nervous wreck and she was shy. Tom made sure that everyone was having fun and letting free. Babiki would always offer me a hug and, on one occasion, a little kiss when we said our goodbyes. Heaven was where I was. "Yeah, I have a girlfriend," I said. Cool.

I began to feel anxious as the dance drew near. I didn't own a vehicle. I had no respectable clothing. I wanted it to be flawless because this was my first time taking out a pretty female.

After my stepfather's garage failed, he relocated his workshop into the home and we moved to Highlands North. In essence, our large yard and garage in the back served as his new workshop. We had at least ten or fifteen cars in the yard, the driveway, and the street at any given time. These were ancient junkers that Abel kept around to work on and cars that were owned by clients. Tom and I were visiting the house one afternoon. When Tom told Abel about my date, Abel chose to be kind. I could need a car for the dance, he added.

We had owned a red Mazda for a long time; it was a complete piece of junk, but it functioned enough. Although I had already rented it, Abel's BMW was the vehicle I truly desired. Like the Mazda, it was outdated and dilapidated, but a bad BMW is still a BMW. I pleaded with him to let me accept it.

"Please let me use the BMW, please."

"There is absolutely no chance."

"Please. The best time of my life is right now. Please. I beseech you.

"No."

"Please."

"No. You are welcome to use the Mazda.

Tom, who is typically the one to hustle and make deals, took over.

He uttered, "Bra Abie." "I don't believe you comprehend. You would understand why this is so crucial if you saw the girl Trevor is accompanying to the dance. Let's agree. You will allow him to take the

BMW if we bring her here and she turns out to be the most gorgeous female you have ever seen.

Abel considered it.

"All right. Deal.

We brought Babiki back to my place after telling her that my parents wanted to meet her at her apartment. After that, we took her to the rear garage where Abel and his men were working. I went over with Tom to introduce them.

"This is Babiki, Abel. This is Abel, Babiki.

As usual, Abel was lovely and had a wide smile.

He said, "Nice to meet you."

They spent a few minutes talking. Babiki and Tom went out. Abel looked across to me.

"Is that the girl?"

"Yes."

"You are welcome to use the BMW."

I was in dire need of clothing as soon as I got the car. With the exception of my Timberlands, everything I owned was garbage, and I was taking out this girl who was really into fashion. Due to my mother's disapproval of spending money on clothing, I was only able to shop at the stores she let me to visit, which limited my options for a wardrobe. I would have to find something to wear when she told me our budget while we were at a discount clothing store.

I didn't know anything about clothing at the time. Powerhouse was a clothing company that embodied my sense of style. It was the type of clothing that weightlifters would wear at Venice Beach or in Miami: loose-fitting sweatshirts and track pants. A cartoon of this enormous bodybuilder bulldog enjoying a cigar, showing off his muscles, and sporting wraparound sunglasses served as the emblem. He was flexing all the way down your leg on the pants. He was flexing across your chest on the shirt. He was flexing on your crotch on the underwear. I can't even pretend that I didn't think Powerhouse was the worst thing ever. I was working because I had no friends, I adored dogs, and I thought muscles were nice. I owned the entire Powerhouse line, including five identical outfits in five different colors. It was simple. I knew how to make it work because the pants were included with the top.

When my CD business's second intermediary, Bongani, learned that I had a date, he decided to give me a makeover. "You have to step it up," he remarked. "For her sake, not yours, you can't attend the dance the way you appear. Let's go shopping.

I went to my mother and pleaded with her for money so that I could get a dancing outfit. At last, she gave in and gave me 2,000 rand for a single outfit. She had never given me that much money for anything in my life. When I informed Bongani how much I needed to spend, he claimed we could figure something out. He informed me that the secret to seeming wealthy is to own one pricey item and then purchase simple, high-quality items for the rest. Everyone will notice the attractive object, giving the impression that you have spent more money than you actually have.

The leather coats that everyone wore in The Matrix were, in my opinion, the coolest thing ever. When The Matrix was released in high school, it was my all-time favorite film. Neo was adored by me. I knew deep down that I was Neo. He is a nerd. He is a badass superhero in secret, yet he is useless at everything. I only needed a strange, bald black man to enter my life and lead the way. "You can do it," said Bongani, who was black and had shaved his head. You are the one. And I said, "Yes." I was aware of it.

I informed Bongani that I wanted the black, ankle-length leather coat that Keanu Reeves wore. Bongani put an end to that. "No, that is not feasible. Although it's cool, you won't be able to wear it ever again. He went me shopping and we got a black leather jacket that was calf length. It would have looked absurd now, but because of Neo, it was really stylish at the time. The cost of it alone was 1,200 rand. We then added a cream-white knitted sweater, suede square-toed shoes, and a pair of basic black pants to complete the ensemble.

Bongani studied my massive Afro for a long time after we got the outfit. I was constantly attempting to achieve the ideal Michael Jackson Afro from the 1970s. I ended up with more Buckwheat, which was like driving a pitchfork into a bed of crabgrass—unruly and hard to comb.

"That fucking hair needs to be fixed," Bongani remarked.

"What do you mean?" "I said." "Just my hair here."

"No, we need to take action."

Alexandra was where Bongani resided. We went to speak with some of the females from his block who were lingering on the corner after he pulled me there.

He asked them, "What would you do with this guy's hair?"

The females examined me.

One of them remarked, "He has so much." "What keeps him from cornrowing it?"

"Shit," they replied. "That's fantastic!"

"What?" I asked. Cornrows? No!

"No," they murmured. "Take action."

I was pulled down the street to a hair parlor by Bongani. We entered and took a seat. After stroking my hair and shaking her head, the woman turned to face Bongani.

She declared, "I can't work with this sheep." "You need to take action on this."

"What should we do?"

"You need to calm things down. That's not what I do here.

"All right."

I was pulled to a second salon by Bongani. The woman took my hair and began painting it with this creamy white substance when I sat down in the chair. My first indication that perhaps this wasn't such a good idea should have been that she was wearing rubber gloves to protect her own skin from the chemical relaxer. She advised me to attempt to keep the relaxer in my hair for as long as possible once it was fully applied. The thing will begin to burn. Tell me when it begins to burn, and we'll rinse it out. However, your hair will become straighter the longer you can tolerate it.

I sat in the chair and waited as long as I could because I wanted to do it correctly.

I was waiting too long.

She had instructed me to notify her as soon as it began to burn. Since it had already removed multiple layers of my scalp by the time it began to burn, she ought to have instructed me to notify her when it began to tingle. When I began to panic, I had long since outgrown the sensation. "It's on fire! It's on fire! After hurrying me to the basin, she began to rinse the relaxer. The chemical doesn't actually begin to burn until it is being washed out, which is something I was unaware of. My head felt like it was being doused with liquid fire. My scalp was covered in regions of acid burns after she was finished.

The salon was filled with women, and I was the only man there. It provided insight into what it's like for women to regularly look good. I wondered why they would ever do this. This is awful. However, it was successful. I had perfectly straight hair. I looked like a pimp, a pimp dubbed Slickback, after the woman combed it back.

The woman consented to cornrow my hair after Bongani pulled me back to the first salon. She worked slowly. Six hours passed. "All right, you can look in the mirror," she finally said. After she spun me around in the chair, I turned to face the mirror and... That was the first time I had ever seen myself like that. It was similar to the makeover parts in my American films, where the swan is transformed from an ugly duckling by fixing their hair and changing their attire. I never tried to look nice for a female since I was so sure I would never get a date, thus I was unaware that I could. The hair looked nice. Although my skin wasn't flawless, it was improving; the pustules had turned into typical pimples. I didn't look too horrible.

My mother shrieked as soon as I entered the house once I got home.

"Oh my god! My newborn boy was transformed into a lovely little lady by them! I have a young girl! You look so lovely!

"Mom! Come on. Put an end to it.

"Are you telling me that you're gay in this manner?"

"What? No. Why would you say that?

"If you are, you know it's okay."

"No, mother. I'm not gay.

My entire family adored it. It looked fantastic to them all. However, my mother did make fun of me.

She remarked, "It's really nicely done, but it's just too pretty." You do appear to be a girl.

Finally, the big night arrived. Tom arrived to assist me in getting ready.

Everything, including the attire and hair, came together flawlessly. After I got ready, we headed to Abel to pick up the BMW's keys, and that's when the entire evening took a turn for the worse.

Since it was the end of the week and a Saturday, Abel was drinking with his employees. As soon as I saw his eyes when I came out to his garage, I knew he was intoxicated. Fuck. Abel was a totally different person when intoxicated.

"Ah, you look nice!" he exclaimed, grinning broadly as he examined me. "Where are you heading?"

"Where am I—I'm heading to the dance, Abie."

"All right. Enjoy yourself.

"May I please have the keys?"

"What are the keys to?"

"To the vehicle."

"What vehicle?"

"The BMW. I could take the BMW to the dance, you said.

He said, "Go buy me some beers first."

Tom and I headed to the booze store after he handed me the keys to his car. I drove back and unloaded everything for Abel after buying him a couple cases of beer.

"All right," I said, "may I now take the BMW?"

"No."

"What does 'no' mean to you?"

"I mean, 'no,' I have to have my car tonight."

However, you made a pledge. I could handle it, you said.

"Yes, but I must have the car."

I was devastated. For about thirty minutes, Tom and I sat there and pleaded with him.

"Please."

"No."

"Please."

"Nope."

At last, we recognized that it would not occur. We traveled to Babiki's residence in the dingy Mazda. I picked her up one hour late. In fact, she was furious. She finally came out after Tom had to go inside and persuade her to do so.

In a stunning red dress, she looked even more stunning than before, but it was obvious that she wasn't feeling well. I smiled and continued to act like a gentleman, holding the door for her and complimenting her on her beauty, even though I was secretly beginning to panic. After saying our goodbyes to Tom and the sister, we left.

Then I lost my way. At one point, I was totally lost and didn't know where I was, and the dance was taking place at a place in an area of town I didn't know. For an hour, I drove about in the dark, doubling back, turning left, and turning right. I spent the entire time on my phone, frantically phoning people, attempting to locate myself, and attempting to obtain directions. Babiki, who was obviously not feeling me or this evening at all, sat beside me in dead silence the entire time. I was crashing hard. I arrived late. I had no idea where I was heading. She had never gone on a date as awful as she did with me.

We arrived at the dance over two hours late after I finally worked out where I was. After parking, I leaped out and hurried to retrieve her door. She just sat there as I opened it.

"Are you prepared?" "I said." "Let's enter."

"No."

"No? What exactly do you mean by "no"?

"No."

"All right, but why?"

"No."

However, we must enter. Inside is the dance.

"No."

For twenty more minutes, I remained there pleading with her to come inside, but she insisted on saying no. She refused to exit the vehicle.

At last, I said, "All right, I'll be right back."

Bongani was inside when I dashed in.

He asked, "Where have you been?"

"I'm present! However, my date is in the car and refuses to enter.

"You mean that she won't enter?"

"I have no idea what's happening. Please assist me.

We returned to the parking area. As soon as he saw her, Bongani lost it. I led him to the car. "Jesus in heaven! I've never seen a more stunning woman than this one. Trevor, you mentioned she was gorgeous, but this is crazy. He abruptly stopped caring about assisting me with Babiki. He called to the boys as he turned and hurried back inside. "Dude! You must attend this! Trevor got a date! She's also stunning! Gentlemen! Come on out here!

A group of twenty men rushed into the parking lot. They huddled close to the vehicle. "She's so gorgeous!" "Dude, did Trevor accompany this girl?" At the zoo, men were staring at her as if she were an animal. They wanted to snap photos with her. Others inside were being called back. "This is crazy! Take a peek at Trevor's date! You must come and see! No, no, no!

I felt ashamed. I had meticulously avoided any romantic humiliation during my four years of high school, but now, on the night of all nights—the matric dance—my humiliation had grown into a circus that was larger than the event itself: We should all go outside and watch since Trevor, the unstoppable clown, is crashing and burning, even though he thought he would have the most beautiful girl at the dance.

Refusing to move, Babiki sat in the passenger seat and stared straight ahead. I was pacing anxiously outside the automobile. One of my friends sneaked a bottle of brandy into the dance. "Have some of this here," he said. I started drinking because, at that point, nothing mattered. I had made a mistake. I was disliked by the girl. The evening was over.

After a while, most of the guys wandered back inside. I was getting intoxicated while sitting on the sidewalk and taking swigs from the brandy bottle. Eventually, Bongani returned to the car to make one final attempt to persuade Babiki to enter. His head appeared above the car with a perplexed expression after a minute.

He said, "Hey, Trevor, your date doesn't speak English."

"What?"

"Your date. She doesn't speak English at all.

"That isn't feasible."

I rose and made my way to the vehicle. She stared at me blankly when I asked her a question in English.

Bongani gave me a glance.

"What prevented you from recognizing that your date is not fluent in English?"

"I'm not sure,"

"Have you not talked to her before?"

"I have, of course, or—wait—have I?"

I began to reminisce about all the times I had spent with Babiki, including our meetings at her apartment, our time spent with her friends, and our introductions to Abel. Then, did I speak to her? No. Then, did I speak to her? No. The scene in which Ed Norton's character flashes back and discovers that he and Brad Pitt had never been in the same room with Helena Bonham Carter simultaneously was reminiscent of the scene from Fight Club. He comes to the realization that he has been punching himself the entire time. His name is Tyler Durden. We never really spoke to each other during the days we spent hanging out and getting to know Babiki, despite the pleasure of meeting her. Tom was always the conduit.

Damn you, Tom.

Tom had assured me that he would find me a lovely date for the dance, but he had not promised anything else about her. She spoke Pedi to Tom and he spoke English to me whenever we were together. I didn't speak Pedi, and she didn't speak English. Pedi was spoken by Abel. He spoke easily with her when they first met because he had studied multiple South African languages to interact with his clients. However, I suddenly realized that I had only ever heard her say "Yes" and "No" in English. "Hello." "Goodbye." That's it: "Yes." "No." "Hello." "Goodbye."

Babiki didn't communicate much in the first place since she was so shy, and I didn't know how to approach her because I was so awkward among women. I didn't even know what a "girlfriend" was; I had never had one. Someone remarked, "She's your girlfriend," and placed a stunning woman on my arm. Her beauty and the mere thought of her had captivated me, and I was unaware that I was meant to speak with her. I had never had to speak with the nude women on my computer, ask them what they thought, or inquire about their emotions. I simply nodded and grinned along with Tom, letting him speak since I was worried that I would say something that would spoil the entire conversation.

Babiki's little sister Lerato spoke a little English, while all three of her older sisters were fluent in the language. As a result, Babiki, her sisters, and their friends spoke English most of the time when we were with them. I never cared because I understood enough of the conversation from everyone's English to understand what was happening, even though the rest of it was passing me by in Pedi or Sotho, which is very usual in South Africa. Additionally, because of the way my mind processes language, even when I hear other languages, they are filtered into English. They are stored in English in my thoughts. It's kept in English, but it happened in Xhosa when my grandmother and great-grandmother were frantically pleading with God to drive out the devil that had pooped on their kitchen floor. It was English, as I recall. Because that's how I recalled it, I felt that Babiki and the times we'd spent together had happened in English whenever I dreamed about her in bed at night. Furthermore, Tom had never mentioned the language she spoke or didn't speak since he didn't think it mattered. All he wanted was to meet the sister and grab his free CDs. This is how I had been seeing a girl for more than a month without ever speaking to her, and I firmly believed that she was my first girlfriend.

From her perspective, I could see why she didn't want to get out of the car, and the entire night suddenly came flooding back. She most likely owed Tom a favor, and Tom has the ability to persuade anyone to do anything, so she probably hadn't wanted to attend the dance with me in the first place. She was furious with me after I left her waiting for me for an hour. She discovered I couldn't even carry on a conversation with her when she got into the car, which was the first time we had ever been by ourselves. She was a young girl alone in a car in the middle of nowhere with an unfamiliar person, and I had no idea where I was driving her. I had drove her about and been lost in the dark. It's likely that she was afraid. She didn't speak anyone's language when we arrived at the dance. She had no acquaintances. I wasn't even familiar to her.

I was standing outside the automobile, looking at Bongani. I was at a loss for what to do. I made an effort to communicate with her in all of my languages. Nothing was successful. Her only language was Pedi. I tried utilizing hand signals to communicate with her since I was so desperate.

"Please. You. Me. Yes, dance inside.
"No."
"Please, dance inside."
"No."

I inquired if Bongani could speak Pedi. He didn't. I dashed into the dance and frantically searched for someone who could speak Pedi so I could persuade her to enter. Are you able to speak Pedi? Are you able to speak Pedi? Are you able to speak Pedi? Pedi was not spoken.

Thus, I was unable to attend my matric dance. I stayed in the parking lot all night save for the three minutes I spent scurrying through it in search of someone who spoke Pedi. I got back into the shabby red Mazda and took Babiki home after the dance. The entire time, we sat in awkward silence.

I parked my car in front of her Hillbrow apartment building, sat down for a while, and attempted to think of a gentlemanly and kind way to end the evening. Then, suddenly, she leaned forward and kissed me. Like, a proper, authentic kiss. It was the type of kiss that helped me forget about the recent catastrophe. I was really perplexed. I had no idea what I was meant to do. She withdrew, and I stared into her eyes, thinking, I don't know how girls function.

I exited the vehicle, approached her, and opened her door. I gave her a final wave as she turned to go after gathering her dress and walking toward her apartment.
"Goodbye."
"Goodbye."

Part III

Every high school student in Germany learns about the Holocaust. not only the facts, but also the how, the why, the seriousness, and the significance of it. Germans are consequently raised to be suitably conscious and contrite. To a certain degree, colonization is treated similarly in British classrooms. The history of the Empire is taught to their children with a sort of disclaimer looming over it. "Well, that was embarrassing, wasn't it?"

That is not how the horrors of apartheid have ever been taught in South Africa. Shame and judgment were not instilled to us. The American method of teaching history was used to instruct us. "There was slavery, then Jim Crow, then Martin Luther King Jr., and now it's done" is how the history of racism is taught in America. For us, it was the same. "Apartheid was not good. The release of Nelson Mandela. Let's go on. A few facts, but never the moral or emotional aspect. The teachers, many of whom were white, appeared to have been given a directive. "Never do anything that will aggravate the children."

Chapter 15: Go Hitler!

Three Chinese children—Bolo, Bruce Lee, and John—transferred to Sandringham when I was in grade nine. Out of a thousand students, they were the only Chinese children in the school. Because he resembled Bolo Yeung from the Jean-Claude Van Damme film Bloodsport, Bolo was given the nickname. The fact that Bruce Lee was indeed Bruce Lee changed our lives. Bruce Lee was a Chinese man who was quiet, attractive, and in excellent physical condition. We thought, "This is magic." Thank you for introducing us to Bruce Lee, Jesus. It was strange because of the other two that John was just John.

Bolo was one of my tuck-shop customers, so I got to know him. The parents of Bolo were pirates by trade. They sold videogames they had pirated at flea markets. Bolo, whose father was a pirate, began peddling pirated PlayStation games around school. After receiving their PlayStation from the kids, he would return it a few days later with a chip that allowed them to play pirated games, which he would subsequently resell. Andrew, a white child and fellow pirate who dealt in bootleg CDs, was a friend of Bolo's. Back when no one had a CD writer at home, Andrew, who was two classes above me, was a true computer nerd.

I heard Andrew and Bolo griping about the black students at school one day when I was making my tuck-shop rounds. They understood that since Andrew and Bolo were too afraid of black people to return to demand payment, they could take their goods, say, "I'll pay you later," and then refuse to pay. "Listen, you shouldn't get upset," I murmured, leaning in to their chat. Black folks don't have any money, so we just attempt to obtain more things for less. But allow me to assist you. I'll act as your go-between. I'll sell the goods you provide me, and I'll take care of collecting the proceeds. You offer me a portion of the sale in exchange. We became partners as soon as they approved of the concept.

I was in the ideal position as the tuck-shop guy. My network was configured. I only needed to tap into it. I was able to save money and upgrade my computer with new parts and additional memory thanks to the money I earned from selling CDs and video games. I learned how to do it from computer whiz Andrew, who also showed me where to find the best deals on parts and how to put them together and fix them. He also showed me where to find rewritable CDs in bulk and how his business operated, including how to download music. Since it was the most costly part, the only thing I was lacking was my own CD writer. A CD writer at the time cost almost 2,000 rand, which was the same as the cost of the entire computer.

For a year, I acted as a go-between for Andrew and Bolo. After that, Bolo dropped out of school, allegedly because his parents had been arrested. I started working for Andrew after that, but he decided to leave the game just before matriculating. He said to me, "You've been a faithful partner, Trevor." He also gave me his CD writer as a token of appreciation. Let's start with the fact that Black people at the time hardly had access to computers. A CD writer, though? It was legendary stuff. It was legendary. Andrew transformed my life the day he handed it to me. I had everything I needed to shut down the bootleg industry because of him: production, sales, and distribution.

Naturally, I was a capitalist. I enjoyed selling things, and I was selling something that no one else could supply and that everyone desired. I got 30 rand, or about $3, for my disks. In the store, a standard CD costs between 100 and 150 rand. People would never again purchase actual CDs after they began purchasing from me because the price was too fantastic.

I had a knack for business, but I didn't know anything about music at the time, which was strange for someone who ran a company that pirated music. My mother's house only permitted Christian music, which is the only music I've ever heard. Since Andrew's CD writer was a 1x CD writer, it copied at the same speed as it played. I would go to my room after school every day and spend five to six hours copying CDs. I hung together old automobile speakers that I had rescued from the junkers Abel kept in the yard to create my own surround-sound system. I didn't actually listen to the CDs for a long time, despite having to sit there while they were playing. I was aware that it was against the dealer's code of conduct to get high on your own.

I could get anything for anyone because of the Internet. I never made musical judgments about other people. I gave you the new Nirvana because you requested it. I got you the new DMX because you requested it. Local South African music was popular, but many were hankering after R&B and hip-hop, two genres of Black American music. Jagged Edge was enormous. 112 was enormous. I sold Montell Jordan in large quantities. Montell Jordan, oh.

I started with a 24k modem and a dial-up connection. An album would take a day to download. However, technology continued to advance, and I continued to make investments in the company. I got a 56k modem instead. I acquired multiple CD writers and speedier CD writers. I began to sell more, duplicate more, and download more. My friends Bongani, who lived in Alex, and Tom, who attended Northview, became my own middleman at that point.

"You know what would make a lot of money?" Bongani asked me one day. Since consumers only want to hear the songs they enjoy, why not compile the finest tracks from several albums onto a single CD rather than copying entire albums? I started creating mix CDs since that seemed like a really good concept. They were well-sold. A few weeks later, Bongani returned and said, "Is it possible to make the tracks fade into each other such that the beat continues and the music seamlessly transitions from track one to track two? It will resemble a DJ performing a whole set all night long. It also seemed like a really good idea. I downloaded an application called "beats per minute," or BPM. I could mix and fade between songs, which is pretty much what a DJ can do live, and it featured a graphical interface that resembled two vinyl records side by side. I began producing party CDs, which also became extremely popular.

The business was flourishing. I was making 500 rand a week by matric, and I was having a blast. In South Africa, there are still maids who make less than that, to put it into perspective. I was living the dream as a sixteen-year-old living at home with no real expenditures, but it's a terrible salary if you're trying to maintain a family.

It was the most liberating thing in the world to have money for the first time in my life. The first thing I discovered about wealth is that it allows you to make decisions. Nobody wants to be wealthy. They desire to have options. You have more options the wealthier you are. That's what money is for.

I went to McDonald's, which gave me a completely new sense of freedom. People in America don't get it, but they go crazy when an American chain opens in a third-world nation. That still holds true now. There was a line around the corner when the first Burger King opened in South Africa last year. It happened. "I have to eat at Burger King," everyone was saying. Did you hear? It originated in America. The amusing thing was that there were just white folks in the line. White people's enthusiasm for Burger King was insane. Black folks said, whatever. Burger King wasn't necessary for Black people. McDonald's and KFC had our hearts. The strange thing about McDonald's is that we were likely aware of it from movies long before it opened. Since McDonald's felt like one of those uniquely American products that couldn't be found anyplace else, we never even imagined that we would ever be able to get one in South Africa. We knew we would adore McDonald's even before we had ever tasted it. More McDonald's restaurants were opened in South Africa than in any other nation at one point. Freedom came with Mandela, and McDonald's arrived with freedom. Shortly after we moved to Highlands North, a McDonald's opened up two streets from our house, but my mom would never pay for us to dine there. I thought, Let's do this with my own money. I threw myself into it. At the time, "large" was the largest size; "supersize" wasn't available. I was so proud with myself that I stepped up to the counter, laid down my money, and said, "I'll have a large number one."

I developed a deep affection for McDonald's. I thought McDonald's tasted like America. America is McDonald's. It looks fantastic when it is advertised. You long for it. You purchase it. It blows your mind the first time you take a taste. It surpasses your expectations. You discover halfway through that it's not as good as it seems. After a few nibbles, you realize that something is seriously amiss. After finishing, you return for more because you miss it so much.

After experiencing American cuisine, I never again ate at home. All I ate was McDonald's. The McDonald's, the McDonald's, the McDonald's. My mother tried to make me dinner every night.
"We're having chicken livers tonight."
"No, I'll have McDonald's instead."
"We're having dog bones tonight."

"I believe I'll choose McDonald's once more."

"We're having chicken feet tonight."

"Hmmmm. All right, I'm in. However, I'm going to McDonald's tomorrow.

I was losing my mind as the money continued coming in. I was so snarky that I purchased a cordless phone. This was before to the widespread use of cellphones. I was able to place the cordless phone outside my window, go two blocks to McDonald's, order my large number one, walk back home, go up to my room, and turn on my computer while simultaneously having a discussion. I was that guy on the street talking to my pal while holding a huge phone to my ear with the antenna completely extended. "Yes, I'm simply heading to McDonald's."

Without Andrew, none of the nice things in life would have occurred. I couldn't have become an expert at music piracy and had an endless McDonald's life without him. His small-scale actions demonstrated to me the significance of empowering the marginalized and destitute following injustice. Andrew was white. Computers, resources, and education were all available to his household. For years, my people were crammed into thatched huts and singing, "Two times two is four," while his people were getting ready to attend college. Six is three times two. "La la la la la." The things his family had taken for granted had not been available to my family. I was naturally good at selling, but where was it going to go me without resources and knowledge? The impoverished are constantly lectured: "Take responsibility for yourself! Make a name for yourself! However, what resources do the impoverished have to start their own businesses?

"Give a man a fish, and he'll eat for a day" is a popular saying. A man can eat for the rest of his life if he learns to fish. "And it would be nice if you gave him a fishing rod" is what they omit. That is the missing portion of the analogy. I discovered for the first time in my life that you need someone from the privileged world to approach you and say, "Okay, here's what you need, and here's how it works," while I was working with Andrew. Without Andrew providing me with the CD writer, my talent alone would have been ineffective. "Oh, that's a handout," they say. No. To make money off of it, I still need to work. But without it, I have no hope.

I was working on a CD in my room one afternoon when Bongani stopped by to retrieve his merchandise. He caught me using my computer to mix tunes.

"This is crazy," he declared. "Are you performing live?"
"Yes."
"You're sitting on a gold mine, Trevor, but I don't think you get it. This must be done for a large audience. You should start doing DJing gigs in the township. Nobody has ever witnessed a DJ performing on a computer.

Alexandra was where Bongani resided. Alexandra is a small, crowded slum remnant from the pre-apartheid era, whereas Soweto is a large, government-planned ghetto. Almost stacked on top of each other were rows and rows of shacks made of corrugated iron and cinder block. Because it has the most outrageous parties and the worst crimes, it is known as Gomorrah.

Alexandra's greatest feature is its street parties. You have a party if you get a tent, set it up in the middle of the road, and take over the street. There are no official guest lists or invitations. Simply telling a few individuals causes word of mouth to spread, drawing a crowd. Permits and the like are nonexistent. You are allowed to host a party in your street if you have a tent. As cars approach the crossroads, the driver will notice the person obstructing their path, shrug, and turn around. No one becomes agitated. The sole restriction is that guests are welcome to attend and share your drink if you have a party in front of their home. Until someone is shot or has a bottle smashed in their face, the festivities continue. If it didn't finish that way, it wasn't a party.

The majority of DJs were only able to spin for a few hours at a time, and their purchasing power was restricted to the quantity of vinyls they could purchase. You may need five or six DJs to keep the dancing going because parties lasted all night. However, Bongani was thrilled to see me mixing because he saw a chance to corner the market because I had a huge hard drive full with MP3s.
He inquired, "How much music do you have?"

"I can play for a week," Winamp says.
"We'll become extremely wealthy."

The summer we graduated from Sandringham, we performed at our first event, a New Year's Eve celebration. Together with Bongani, I took my tower, enormous monitor, keyboard, mouse, and all of the wires. After packing everything onto a minibus, we drove it to Alex. People arrived after we occupied the street in front of his house, turned off the electricity, set up the computer, installed speakers, and borrowed a tent. It was explosive. The entire street was crowded from end to end by midnight. That year, we had the largest New Year's Eve celebration in Alexandra, and throwing the largest party in Alexandra is no laughing matter. People continued to arrive from all directions throughout the night. Word got out: "A light-skinned man uses a computer to play music." It is unlike anything you have ever seen. Up until sunrise, I DJed alone. My pals and I were so worn out and inebriated by that point that we passed out on the grass outside Bongani's house. The gathering was so large that it immediately enhanced our reputation in the neighborhood. Before long, we had reservations everywhere.

Bongani and I were unable to get employment after high school. We were unable to find employment. My sole sources of income were CD piracy and DJing events; after leaving Sandringham, the only people who would buy my CDs were the corner kids and minibus drivers in Alexandra. I naturally went there to continue making money because that's where I was playing the most gigs. I knew a lot of white youngsters who were taking a year off. "I plan to travel to Europe during my year off." The white children were saying that. Thus, I declared, "I will also take a year off." I plan to visit the municipality and spend a year hanging out on the corner. And I did just that.

Every day, Bongani, myself, and our team would go sit on the low brick wall that ran down the center of the road in front of Bongani's house in Alex. I would bring my CDs. We would practice dance routines while listening to music. We DJ'd parties at night and hustled CDs all day. We began receiving bookings for performances in different hoods and slums.

I was able to access exclusive music that were only available to a select few thanks to my computer and modem, but it was a challenge for me. At gatherings, I occasionally played the newest music, and guests would occasionally ask, "What is this? To it, how do you dance? For instance, "Watch Me (Whip/Nae Nae)" is a great tune, but what exactly is a whip? What does a DJ play? A nae nae: what is it? You must be able to do the whip and nae nae for that song to be well-liked; new music only works at parties if guests can dance to it. In order to teach people the moves to the music we were playing, Bongani determined that we required a dance crew. Our team from the corner became our dancers because they already knew all the songs because we spend our days listening to CDs and thinking up dancing techniques. And without a doubt, Bongani's neighbor Hitler was the crew's best, most attractive, and most elegant dancer.

I was friends with Hitler, and my goodness, what a dancer he was. It was captivating to see him. Imagine if a jellyfish could walk on ground. That's how free and fluid he was, defying the laws of physics. Tall, lean, and strong, with gorgeous, smooth skin, large teeth, a wonderful smile, and a constant laugh, he was also incredibly attractive. The only thing he did was dance. He would get up early, practice his routines all day, and listen to hip-hop or house music.
Everyone in the hood is aware of the crew's top dancer. He serves as a status symbol for you. You don't have fancy clothes or automobiles when you're poor, yet the finest dancer attracts girls, so you want to hang out with him. We had Hitler. There were dance competitions during the parties. Every neighborhood's children would come and perform their best dances. Hitler was constantly brought in by us, and he nearly always prevailed.

There was no doubt who would be the main attraction as Bongani and I prepared a routine for our dancing crew. The entire set was constructed around Hitler. The dancers would perform a couple of numbers after I warmed up the audience with a few songs. They would spread out to form a semicircle around the stage after the party had begun, leaving a space in the back for Hitler to enter. I would start energizing the audience even more by turning up Redman's "Let's Get Dirty." "Are you prepared? You are not audible to me! Listen to you create some sound! Hitler would leap into the center of the semicircle when the throng began to scream, and the crowd would go crazy. The men would circle around Hitler, encouraging him as he went about his business. " Hit-ler, go! Hit-ler, go! Hit-ler, go! Hit-ler, go! The team would also execute the hip-hop dance, which involves putting your arm out in front of you and bopping it up and down to the beat while keeping your palm flat. Hit-ler, go! Hit-ler, go! Hit-ler, go! Hit-ler, go! A thousand people would be chanting along with their fists raised in the air, and the entire crowd would be in a frenzy. "Go, Hit-ler! Hit-ler, go! Hit-ler, go! Hit-ler, go!

Hitler is hardly unheard of in South Africa, despite his unique moniker. It's partly related to the way many Black people choose their names. Black people take considerable care while selecting their traditional names, which have very particular connotations. However, black individuals in South Africa were forced to have an English or European name as well, one that white people could essentially pronounce, from colonial times through the apartheid era. Thus, Patricia Nombuyiselo Noah was your last name, English name, and traditional name. Most of the time, your European name was picked at random, borrowed from the Bible, or derived from a well-known politician or Hollywood star. I know men with Napoleon and Mussolini names. And Hitler, of course.

That shocks and perplexes Westerners, but in reality, the West is reaping the consequences of its actions. Africa was divided by the colonial powers, who also forced the Black man to labor and failed to provide him with a good education. Black people and white folks don't communicate. Why, then, would Black people be aware of what is happening in the world of white people? As a result, a large portion of South Africa's black population is largely unaware of Hitler. "A hitler" was viewed by my own grandfather as a type of army tank that was aiding the Germans in winning the war. Because he interpreted what he heard on the news in that way. The narrative of the war for many black South Africans was that the Allies were losing because of a figure named Hitler. Hitler was so strong that black people eventually had to go battle him alongside white people. If a white man had to go to such lengths as to ask a black man for assistance in a fight, that person must be the hardest person in history. Thus, you name your dog Hitler if you want him to be tough. You name your child

Hitler if you want them to be tough. It's likely that you have an uncle named Hitler. It's only a thing.

Though only in a fundamental sense, we learned more about World War II at Sandringham than the average black child in the townships. Critical thinking concerning Hitler, anti-Semitism, and the Holocaust was not taught to us. For example, we were not taught that the racist policies of the Third Reich served as some inspiration for the apartheid architects, who were avid supporters of Hitler. Hitler's relationship to the world we lived in was not conveyed to us. Simply put, we weren't being taught to think. We were only taught that Hitler invaded Poland in 1939, the Soviet Union in 1941, and then something else in 1943. They are merely facts. Write them down for the test, commit them to memory, and then forget about them.

There's also this to think about: Because Hitler is not the worst thing a black South African could conceive, the name Hitler does not anger them. Every nation, particularly those in the West, believes that its history is the most significant. Cecil Rhodes, however, would emerge before Hitler if black South Africans could travel back in time and murder one person. King Leopold of Belgium would be well ahead of Hitler if Congolese people could travel back in time and murder just one person. Native Americans would most likely murder Andrew Jackson or Christopher Columbus if they could travel back in time and murder only one person.
 I frequently encounter Westerners who unquestioningly maintain that the Holocaust was the greatest atrocity in human history. It was awful, really. However, I frequently ponder how horrifying African massacres, such as those in the Congo, were. Documentation is something the Jews have that Africans have not. The Nazis made films, took photographs, and kept exacting records. And it really boils down to that. Hitler counted Holocaust victims, so they do. Six million people were slaughtered. We may all be appalled by that figure, and with good reason. However, there are no statistics—just educated guesses—when you read about the history of horrors committed against Africans. Being terrified by a guess is more difficult. Portugal and Belgium did not count the number of Black people they killed when they pillaged Angola and the Congo. In the Congo, how many Black people lost their lives while harvesting

rubber? In the Transvaal's diamond and gold mines?

Hitler is, therefore, the greatest madman in history in both Europe and America. He is just another historical strongman in Africa. I never once wondered myself, "Why is his name Hitler?" during the entire time I spent with him. He was given the name Hitler by his mother.

We really took off after Bongani and I included dancers in our DJ performances. Our group was known as the Black and White Boys. The Springbok Boys were the name of the dancers. We began to receive reservations everywhere. Even though many black families were relocating to the suburbs, their children still wanted to host block parties and maintain ties to the township culture, so they hired us to perform at their gatherings. Word spread. Before long, we had a growing number of suburban bookings, performing for and meeting white people.

The mother of a young person we met from the area was active in developing cultural activities for educational institutions. They would be referred to as "diversity programs" in America. They were spreading throughout South Africa because, in this post-apartheid period, we were meant to be loving and learning about each other. The mother of this child asked us whether we would want to perform at a cultural event at a school in Linksfield, a posh neighborhood south of Sandringham where my friend Teddy had resided. There would be a variety of dances and musical styles, and everyone would gather to socialize and celebrate their culture. We accepted her offer to pay. She emailed us the details, including the school's name (King David School), time, and location. a school for Jews.

We reserved a minibus, packed it with our belongings, and traveled over on the day of the event. After arriving, we sat in the rear of the school's assembly hall to watch the performers who came onstage before us. Flamenco dancers, Greek dancers, and traditional Zulu musicians were among the groups who took turns performing. After that, we got up. We were referred to as the South African B-Boys, or Hip Hop Pantsula Dancers. Onstage, we set up our sound system. When I peeked out, the entire hall was filled with Jewish children, all dressed in yarmulkes, getting ready for a celebration.

I took the microphone. "Are you prepared to rock?!"

"Yes, indeed!"

"Create some sound!"

"Yes, indeed!"

I began to play. Everyone was having a blast, my gang was dancing, and the bass was thumping. Hundreds of children, parents, teachers, and chaperones were all dancing wildly. Our act was supposed to last fifteen minutes, and around the ten-minute mark, I had to pull out my star dancer, play "Let's Get Dirty," and shut up.

I took the mic, the dancers formed a semicircle, and I began the song. "Are you all prepared?!"

"Yes, indeed!"

"You people aren't prepared! Are you prepared?

"Yeeeaaahhhhhhhh!"

"All   right!   Make   some   noise   for HIIIIIITTTTLLLLLEERRRRR-RRRRR- and give it up!

Hitler leaped to the center of the circle and began murdering it. "Go Hit-ler! Go Hit-ler! Go Hit-ler! Go Hit-ler!" was the shout of the guys surrounding him. They were jumping to the beat with their arms extended in front of them. "Go, Hit-ler, Go, Hit-ler, Go, Hit-ler!" And I was right there, guiding them with the microphone. "Go, Hit-ler, Go, Hit-ler, Go, Hit-ler!"

The room came to a halt. There was no dancing. The hundreds of Jewish children in their yarmulkes, the parents, the teachers, and the chaperones all froze and gaped at us up on stage. I didn't know. Hitler was, too. We continued. The music's beat and my voice on the microphone shouting, "Go Hit-ler!" were the only sounds in the room for at least thirty seconds. Hit-ler, go! Hit-ler, go! For Hitler, raise your hands in the air!

A instructor rushed up behind me and pulled my system's plug from the wall. She turned on me and became furious when the hall fell silent. "You dare! This is abhorrent! You dreadful, repulsive, vile thing! You dare!

As I tried to understand what she was talking about, my mind was racing. Then it made sense. O spana va was a unique dance move that Hitler used. It was quite sexual and meant "where you work": He would push and gyrate his hips as if he were fucking the air. He was making that move as the teacher went out, so it's obvious that the dance was what she found so repulsive. However, this was a common shift among Africans. It's ingrained in our culture. This woman called us repulsive when we were celebrating a cultural day and showcasing our culture. She took offense, and her taking offense upset me.

I said, "Lady, I think you should relax."
"I refuse to relax! You have no right to insult us here!
"No one is being insulted by this. This is who we are!
"Leave this place! You folks are abhorrent.
And there it was. You folks. I realized now that this woman was prejudiced. She was unable to see black men dance provocatively without becoming enraged. We continued to argue as I began packing up my equipment.
"Listen, lady. We are now at liberty. We will do what we are going to do. We can't be stopped.
"I'll let you know that we can stop you again because my people have stopped people like you in the past."
Naturally, she was discussing halting the Nazis during World War II, but it wasn't what I heard. In South Africa, Jews are simply white people. All I could hear was a white woman yelling that white people had previously beaten us and would do so again. I answered, "Lady, you will never stop us again." This is where I pulled out the trump card: "Now that Nelson Mandela is on our side, you will never stop us! And he assured us that we could succeed!
"What?"
She was very perplexed. I'd had enough. I began to curse at her. "Dude, screw you. Screw your program. Screw your school. Fuck your entire population. Guys, let's go! We're leaving!

We didn't leave that school on foot. We danced away. We pumped our fists in the air as we danced along the street. "Go, Hit-ler, Go, Hit-ler, Go, Hit-ler!" since Hitler had put an end to it. Those white people had no idea what hit them when Hitler performed the most gangster dance movements ever.

Chapter 16: The Cheese Boys

Bongani, my friend, was a short, bald, and extremely buff man. That wasn't always the case with him. He had always been thin, but his life was completely turned upside down when he came upon a bodybuilding magazine. Bongani was one of those individuals who made everyone feel their best. The reason so many of the township kids attracted toward him—and me, too—was because he was that friend who saw your potential and believed in you when no one else did. Although Bongani had always been well-liked, his reputation truly took off once he physically assaulted one of the school's most notorious bullies. That solidified his position as the township children's guardian and leader.

While we were still in school, Bongani lived in Alex, but I never went there; instead, he would constantly come to my house in Highlands North. Although I had visited Alex a few times for short stays, I had never stayed for an extended period of time. To put it that way, I had never visited there at night. There are differences between visiting Alex during the day and at night. There was a reason the place was called Gomorrah.

Shortly before we matriculated, Bongani approached me on the quad one day after school.

He said, "Hey, let's head to the hood."

"The hood?"

I didn't understand what he was talking about at first. Although I was familiar with the many townships where Black people resided and had heard the term "hood" in rap music, I had never used either term to refer to the other.

As American hip-hop was exploding and hip-hop made it cool to be from the hood, the walls of apartheid were falling. Living in a township used to be the lowest of the lowest and something to be ashamed of. Then came films like Menace II Society and Boyz n the ghetto, which made the ghetto seem hip. It belonged to the characters in such films and songs. Children in the townships began to follow suit, wearing their identity like a badge of honor: You were from the hood now, not the township. You had far more street cred if you were from Alex than if you lived in Highlands North. I wanted to know what Bongani meant when he stated, "Let's go to the hood." I was curious to learn more.

As is customary, we entered from the Sandton side when Bongani took me to Alex. You pass opulent mansions and enormous sums of money as you travel through one of Johannesburg's wealthiest areas. After that, you pass through Wynberg's industrial belt, which separates the wealthy and white from the impoverished and black. The bus terminal and the enormous minibus rank are located at the entrance to Alex. The busy, chaotic third-world bazaar is similar to what you see in the James Bond and Jason Bourne films. It's the outside version of Grand Central Station. Everything is changing. Everything is moving. It appears the same every day, yet nothing feels like it was there yesterday or that it will be there tomorrow.

You're in Alex proper once you pass the minibus rank. There aren't many locations I've been with electricity like Alex does. All day long, it's a bustling hub of human activity, with people coming and going, gangsters working, men sitting on the street doing nothing, and children playing. All of that energy has nowhere to go and no way to release itself, so it occasionally explodes in violent outbursts and wild parties. The next thing you know, a police car is chasing gangsters through the streets, a gunfight is taking place, and helicopters are buzzing overhead. One minute it will be a calm afternoon with people hanging around and going about their daily business. Ten minutes later, it seems as though nothing happened; everyone is back to their usual activities, including running around and hanging out.

Alex is arranged like a grid, with several avenues. Although the walkways are primarily made of dirt, the streets are paved. The gray and dark gray corrugated iron and cinder block color pattern is broken up by vibrant bursts of color. Perhaps someone picked up a bright-blue piece of sheet metal by chance, or someone painted a lime green wall, or there's a bright-red sign above a takeout restaurant. Basic sanitary facilities are scarce. There is trash all over the place, usually a garbage fire burning down a side street. Something is constantly burning in the hood.

You can smell every conceivable scent as you stroll. In the streets, people are preparing meals and ordering takeout. The water system has backed up again, so the family who lives in a shack that was jury-rigged onto the back of someone else's shack has no running water, so they take a bucket bath from the outdoor tap and then dump the dirty water in the street, where it flows into the existing sewerage river. A guy who fixes cars acts as like he understands what he's doing, but he doesn't. A river of filth is flowing down the street as a result of him pouring old motor oil into it and the oil mixed with the unclean bathwater. A goat is always present, so it's likely that one is hanging around. You hear the constant hum of human activity as you walk—people conversing in a dozen different languages, arguing, negotiating, and chatting. Music is playing all the time. One corner is filled with traditional South African music, the next is Dolly Parton, and the Notorious B.I.G. is being pumped by a car passing by.

For me, the hood was a total sensory overload, but amidst the mayhem, there was structure, order, and a social hierarchy according to residence. Because First Avenue was so close to the chaos of the minibus rank, it was not cool at all. The semi-houses on Second Avenue were constructed when some kind of official settlement was still in progress, which made it a pleasant avenue. For the township, Third, Fourth, and Fifth Avenues were prettier. These were the old money, the well-established families. From Sixth Avenue onward, the area became increasingly shabby, with more shacks and shanties. A few soccer fields and schools were present. The government constructed a number of enormous constructions, known as hostels, to house migrant labor. You had no desire to visit the place. The serious gangsters were there. Only if you had to purchase an AK-47 did you go there.

The newest and prettiest area of the neighborhood, East Bank, was located over the Roosevelt Street Bridge on the far side of the Jukskei River, which you reach after Twentieth Avenue. The government had moved into the East Bank, evicted the squatters and their shacks, and began constructing real houses. Though these were decent two-bedroom homes with little yards, the housing was still low-income. Families with some money typically sent their children to better schools, such as Sandringham, outside of the neighborhood. After walking through the ghetto from the minibus rank, we ended up outside Bongani's parents' house on the low brick wall down the center of Springbok Crescent, doing nothing but shooting the shit. Bongani's parents lived in East Bank, near the junction of Roosevelt and Springbok Crescent. I had no idea at the time that I would be spending the next three years of my life there.

By the time I graduated from high school at the age of seventeen, my stepfather had made my home life toxic. My mother agreed with me that I should leave since I no longer wanted to be there. She assisted me in relocating to a cheap apartment in a building down the street that was plagued with roaches. If I had a plan, it was to attend college and become a computer programmer, but we couldn't pay the tuition. I had to earn money. I only knew how to make money by selling unlicensed CDs, and since the minibus rank was in the hood, that was one of the finest areas to sell CDs. Because they employed good music to draw consumers, minibus drivers were constantly searching for new songs.

The hood's affordability was another appealing feature. You can survive on almost nothing. A kota is a type of food that is available in the neighborhood. The bread is a quarter loaf. The bread is scraped out and then filled with fried potatoes, achar (a pickled mango relish), and a slice of baloney. A few rand are spent on that. You can purchase more enhancements the more money you have. You can add a hot dog if you have a little extra cash. If you have a little extra, you may add a fried egg or a genuine sausage, such as a bratwurst. With all the improvements, the largest one can feed three people.

The best improvement, in our opinion, was adding a piece of cheese. Due to its high cost, cheese was always the preferred option. The hood ran on the cheese standard, so forget about the gold standard. Anything with cheese was profitable. It was nice if you received a burger, but if you got a cheeseburger, you were richer than a man who only had a hamburger. If you had cheese in your refrigerator or on a sandwich, you were enjoying the good life. People would say, "Oh, you're a cheese boy," if you had some money in any South African ghetto. In summary, just because your family can afford cheese doesn't mean you're truly hood.

Bongani and his team were regarded as cheese boys in Alex since they resided in the East Bank. Ironically, the kids in the better homes higher up in East Bank were the cheesier cheese boys, and they were despised as the scumbags of the neighborhood since they lived on the first block just over the river. Bongani and his team would never acknowledge that they were cheeseboys. "We're not cheese," they would say. We are a hood. "Eh, you're not hood," the true hood dudes would respond. You're a piece of cheese. As they pointed farther up East Bank, Bongani's men would remark, "We're not cheese." "They're cheese." There was a lot of absurd posturing about who was cheese and who was hood.

As his crew's captain, Bongani was the one who brought everyone together and got things going. And then there was Bongani's goon, Mzi. The little boy merely wanted to join in and be part of the group. Bheki was our go-to person for beverages; he would always locate us alcohol and create a reason to have some. Then Kakoatse appeared. We referred to him as G. Mr. Nice Guy. G was just interested in ladies. He was in the game if women were involved. Finally, the life of the party, Hitler, appeared. Hitler merely desired to dance.

When apartheid fell, cheese lads found themselves in a particularly precarious position. Being born in the hood and knowing that you will always be there is one thing. However, the outside world has been exposed to the cheese guy. His family has fared well. They own a home. They may have even matriculated him, as they had sent him to a respectable school. Although his potential has increased, he has not been given more opportunities. Although he has been made aware of the world outside, he has not been provided with the means to access it.

Technically speaking, South Africa's unemployment rate was "lower" during apartheid, which makes sense. Slavery existed; everyone was employed in this way. Everyone was required to get a minimum wage when democracy arrived. When labor costs increased, millions of individuals found themselves unemployed. After apartheid, young Black men's jobless rates skyrocketed, occasionally reaching 50%. Many men find that after high school, they are unable to pay for college, and even small retail jobs might be difficult to find if you're from the neighborhood and have a particular appearance and speech pattern. Therefore, freedom for many young men in South Africa's townships means that they wake up every morning, regardless of whether their parents are at work or not. After that, they head outdoors and spend the entire day chatting trash on the corner. They have been taught how to fish and are free, but nobody is willing to give them a fishing pole.

I discovered early on in the hood that the distinction between criminal and civilian life is quite thin. We prefer to think that there are good and terrible people in the world, and it's easier to think that in the suburbs because it's hard to get to know a career criminal there. However, when you visit the hood, you discover that there are a lot of different tints.

Gangsters were your neighbors and pals in the hood. You were familiar with them. You saw them at parties and spoke with them on the street. You had them in your world. Before they were gangsters, you knew them. "Hey, that's a crack dealer," was not the statement. "Oh, little Jimmy's selling crack now," it was. The strange thing about these gangsters was that they all looked the same at first glance. Their red sports vehicle was identical. The same stunning eighteen-year-old girls were their dates. It was odd. They seemed to share a personality rather than having distinct personas. It's possible that one is the other and the other is the one. Each of them had studied the ways of that thug.

Even if you're not a serious criminal, crime is a part of your life in the neighborhood. It comes in different levels. From the mom buying food that fell off the back of a truck to feed her family to the gangs selling military-grade hardware and guns, it involves everyone. I learned from the hood that crime thrives because it cares, which is the one thing the government doesn't do. Crime starts at the local level. Crime targets young children who require assistance and a helping hand. Crime provides summer employment, internships, and career progression possibilities. The community becomes involved with crime. There is no discrimination in crime.

I began my criminal career by peddling pirated CDs on the street. Even if it wasn't illegal by hood standards, I feel like I owe all these artists money for taking their music, even though that was a crime in and of itself. None of us realized at the time that we were doing anything improper; after all, why would they create CD writers if copying CDs is wrong?

Bongani's home had a garage that looked out onto Springbok Crescent. We would put up a table, play music, open the doors, and run an extension cord out onto the street each morning. As they passed, people would inquire, "What is that? Would you just give me one? Numerous minibus drivers terminated their runs at our corner and circled back to the minibus rank. They would stop by, place their order, return, and pick it up. Stop by, place your order, then return to pick it up. We ran out to them all day, returned to the garage to prepare more concoctions, and then went out to sell again. When we were sick of the wall, we would hang out in the converted shipping container around the corner. We would utilize the pay phone that was located inside to make phone calls. We would move back and forth between the wall and the container when business was sluggish, chatting and socializing with the other folks who had nothing better to do during the day. We would converse with criminals and drug dealers. Occasionally, the police would burst through. A typical day in the neighborhood. The same thing the following day.

Because Bongani spotted all the opportunities and knew how to take advantage of them, selling gradually turned into hustling. Bongani was a hustler, just like Tom. Bongani, on the other hand, had schemes: If we do this, we acquire that, then we can flip that for the other thing, which gives us the leverage we need to achieve something greater. Tom, on the other hand, was just concerned with the short con. For instance, several minibus drivers were unable to make upfront payments. They would say, "I just started my shift, so I don't have the money." However, I need fresh music. Is there any way I could give you guys credit? You'll have to pay me. When my shift is over and the week is over, I'll pay you. We therefore began allowing drivers to make purchases on credit, although with a small interest charge.

We began to earn more money. It was always cash on hand, never more than a few hundred or perhaps a thousand rand at a time. Bongani quickly recognized our predicament. The one item that everyone in the neighborhood needs is cash. To pay a bill, pay a fine, or simply keep things together, everyone is searching for a short-term loan. People began approaching us and requesting cash. After making a contract,

Bongani would approach me. "Hey, let's work out a deal with this person. We will lend him one hundred dollars, and at the end of the week, he will return one twenty. Alright, I would say. The man would then return and offer us 120 rand. Then we repeated it. Then we repeated the process. First, we doubled our money, and then we tripled it.

We also had leverage in the barter economy of the hood thanks to cash. People will try to sell you something if you're standing on a corner of a main street in the neighborhood, as everyone knows. Man, yo, yo, yo. Do you want some cannabis? "Want to purchase a VCR?" "Want to purchase a DVD player?" "Hey, I'm a TV seller." That's the way it is.

Assume that two men are negotiating on the corner: a crackhead attempting to sell a DVD player, and a working man who wants one but lacks the funds because he hasn't received his paycheck yet. The crackhead wants the money now, but they are back and forth. Crackheads are impatient. When dealing with a crackhead, there is no layaway plan. Bongani intervenes and pulls the laborer away.

Bongani explains, "Look, I know you can't afford the DVD player right now." "How much are you willing to spend on it, though?"

He says, "I'll pay one-twenty."

"All right, cool."

The crackhead is then pushed aside by Bongani.

"What is your desired price for the DVD player?"

"I would like forty."

"All right, pay attention. You're a crazy person. This DVD player was stolen. I'll give you fifty dollars.

After a brief period of resistance, the crackhead takes the money because, well, he's a crackhead and crack is all about the moment. Bongani then returns to the working man.

"All right. One-twenty is what we'll do. Your DVD player is here. You own it.

"But the one-twenty isn't with me."

It's awesome. You can have it now, but when you receive your pay, give us one forty instead of one twenty.

"All right."

We now have 140 rand from the working man after investing 50 rand with the crackhead. However, Bongani would figure out how to turn it around and increase it once more. Assume that the person who purchased the DVD player was employed at a shoe store.

"With your staff discount, how much do you spend on a pair of Nikes?" Bongani would inquire.

"I can purchase a pair of Nike sneakers for fifty dollars."

"All right, we'll give you ten instead of one forty, and you can use your discount to get us a pair of Nikes."

Now, this guy is leaving with ten rand in his pocket and a DVD player. He believes he got a fair bargain. We go to one of the cheesier cheese boys up in East Bank after he gets us the Nikes, and we tell him, "Hey, dude, we know you want the new Jordans." The stores have three hundred of them. You can purchase them from us for two hundred dollars. We went ahead and converted 60 rand into 200 after selling him the sneakers.

The hood is that. There are always buyers and sellers, and the hustle is all about trying to be in the center of it. It was all illegal. No one knew the origin of anything. Did the person who purchased our Nikes actually have a "staff discount"? You're not sure. You don't inquire. "Hey, look what I found" and "Cool, how much do you want?" are all that are said. The international code is that.

I didn't know not to ask at first. We once purchased a car stereo or something similar, I recall.

"But who was the owner of this?" I asked.

One of the guys told me, "Well, don't worry about it." "White people are insured."

"Insurance?"

Indeed, white individuals have insurance policies that cover their losses in cash, making it seem as though they haven't lost anything.

"Oh, all right," I replied. "That sounds good."

And that was all we ever considered: White people get money when they lose things, which is simply another pleasant benefit of being white.

When you live in a society that is wealthy enough to be isolated from crime, it is simple to be critical of it. However, the hood made me realize that everyone has a different idea of what is right and wrong, what is considered a crime, and how much crime they are prepared to do. The poor mom isn't thinking, "I'm aiding and abetting a criminal by buying these Corn Flakes boxes," when a crackhead shows up with a crate of them that he stole from the back of a supermarket. No. She purchases the corn flakes because she thinks, "My family needs food, and this guy has corn flakes."

I will never forget the day I came home to find a huge box of frozen burger patties—like two hundred of them—from a takeout restaurant called Black Steer in the kitchen. My own mother, who was very pious and law-abiding and used to shit on me about breaking the laws and learning to behave. At Black Steer, a burger costs at least twenty rand.

"What on earth is this?" "I said."

She remarked, "Oh, some guy at work had these and was selling them." "I received a fantastic discount."

"But from where did he obtain it?"

"I'm not sure. He claimed to know someone who—

"He stole it, Mom."

"We are unaware of that."

"We are aware of that. How on earth is this person going to acquire all these burger patties at random?

We ate the burgers, of course. After that, we gave thanks to God for the dinner.

I assumed we would sell CDs and host DJ parties in the hood when Bongani originally told me, "Let's go to the hood." We discovered that we were DJing parties and selling CDs to fund a pawnshop and payday loan business in the neighborhood. That swiftly became our main line of work.

It was the same every day in the hood. I would get up early. After Bongani picked me up at my apartment, we would take a minibus to Alex, where I would be bringing my computer along with the enormous tower and the bulky, heavy display. We would start the first batch of CDs and set everything up in Bongani's garage. We would then go for a walk. For breakfast, we would head to the intersection of Roosevelt and Nineteenth. Food is where you need to exercise caution while trying to make ends meet. You will lose your gains if you don't plan. We therefore have vetkoek, or fried dough, for breakfast every morning. They were inexpensive—about 50 cents each. We would have enough energy to last us till later in the day if we purchased a number of those.

We would then eat while sitting in the corner. We would be taking orders from the minibus drivers as they passed by while we were eating. We would then return to Bongani's garage to create the CDs, do weights, and listen to music. The drivers would begin returning from their morning trips about ten or eleven. After taking the CDs, we would go to the corner so they could retrieve their belongings. After that, we would simply be sitting out on the corner, interacting with locals, seeing who passed by, and determining the course of the day. This is necessary for a man. That is being sold by a man. You had no idea what it would be.

At lunch, there was always a huge influx of business. We would be visiting various stores and nooks across Alexandra, negotiating with everyone. The minibus drivers would give us free rides if we got on with them and used the ride as a chance to discuss what music they needed, but in reality, we were getting free rides with the guy. "Hey, we would like to get orders. We'll converse while you're behind the wheel. What are you in need of? What kind of music are you seeking? Is the new Maxwell necessary? All well, the new Maxwell arrived. All right, we will speak with you later. Here, we'll leap out. After that, we would board another transport to get to our next destination.

Business would slow down after midday, so we would have our lunch—typically the cheapest item we could get, such as a smiley with some corn meal. The head of a goat is a smiling. After boiling, they are topped with chili pepper. Because the goat appears to be grinning at you from the dish after you've finished eating all the meat off it, we call them smileys. The eyes are repulsive, but the cheeks and tongue are lovely. They burst in your mouth. When you bite the eyeball after putting it in your mouth, it just explodes as a ball of pus. It lacks crunch. It doesn't chew. There is absolutely nothing pleasant about its flavor.

We would return to the garage after lunch to unwind, sleep off our food, and create more CDs. We would see a lot of mothers in the afternoons. Our mothers cherished us. They were among our most loyal clients. Moms are the ones who are looking to buy that box of soap that dropped off the back of the truck because they are the ones who manage the family, and they were more likely to buy it from us than from a crackhead. Crackheads are unpleasant to deal with. We were good-natured, articulate East Bank boys. Because we gave the transaction an extra degree of credibility, we could even charge more. In order to cover this or that for the family, mothers are frequently the ones who want short-term loans the most. Once more, they would prefer to work with us rather than a crooked loan shark. Moms were aware that if they couldn't pay, we wouldn't break anyone's legs. We didn't think that was true. Let's not forget that we weren't able to do it either. But Bongani's genius stepped in at that point. He was always aware of what someone could offer while they were not paying.

Some of the most bizarre trades were made by us. In the neighborhood, mothers are fiercely protective of their daughters, particularly if they are attractive. Some of the girls in Alex were imprisoned. They left for school, arrived home, and entered the house right away. They were not permitted to go. Boys were forbidden from interacting with them or even just being around the house. A guy would constantly talk about a female who was locked away, saying things like, "She's so beautiful." I'll stop at nothing to win her over. However, he was unable to. No one was able to.

That mother would then require a loan. She was unable to evict us from her home once we lent her the money until she reimbursed us. We would stop by, visit, and engage in small talk. The mother couldn't yell, "Don't talk to those boys!" even though the daughter would be right there. We were able to build a relationship with the mother thanks to the financing. We would receive an invitation to remain for dinner. The mother would allow us to take her daughter to a party as long as we assured her that we would bring her home safely after she realized we were kind, decent men. We would then approach the man who had been so eager to meet the daughter.

"Hey, let's work something out. You get to hang out with the girl when we bring her to your party. How much are you able to provide us?

He would say, "I have some cases of beer, but I don't have any money."

"All right, so we're attending this party tonight. For the party, you provide us with two cases of beer.

"Nice."

We would then attend the celebration. The daughter, who was normally overjoyed to get out of her mother's jail, would accept our invitation. We would write off the mom's debt to thank her, the guy would deliver the beer, he would get to hang out with the girl, and we would recoup our costs by selling the drink. It was always possible to find a solution. Working out the angles, figuring out the puzzle, figuring out who needs what, and figuring out who we can connect with to get us the money was frequently the most enjoyable part.

We most likely had about 10,000 rand in capital at the height of our enterprise. We had interest coming in and loans going out. We had our collection of DVD players and Jordans that we had purchased to resale. In addition, we had to rent minibuses to get to our DJ jobs, buy blank CDs, and feed five guys three times a day. We used the computer to keep track of everything. I was familiar with spreadsheets because I grew up in my mother's environment. We prepared a Microsoft Excel document that included each person's name, amount owing, payment date, and nonpayment date.

Business started to pick up after work. Men returning home from work, minibus drivers picking up a final order. The men weren't searching for Corn Flakes and soap. They desired the equipment, including PlayStation games, CD players, and DVD players. Since they had been out working and robbing all day, more men would come in selling goods as well. There would be a man selling shoes, a man selling leather jackets, and another man selling a telephone. There was this one guy who resembled Mr. Burns from The Simpsons in black. He would consistently arrive at the end of his shift with the most bizarre, useless items, such as an electric toothbrush that was disconnected from its charger. He once brought an electric razor to us.

"What on earth is this?"

Is that an electric razor, then?

"A razor that is electric? We're Black. Are you aware of the damage these substances cause to our skin? Is there anybody here who knows how to use an electric razor?

We had no idea where he was getting this information. since you don't inquire. However, we eventually put it together: He was employed at the airport. He was boosting people's luggage, and it was all garbage.

We would wind down as the rush gradually started to wear off. We would balance our accounts, review our CD stock, and make our final collections. We would begin preparing if there was a party to DJ that evening. If not, we'd purchase a couple drinks, relax, chat about the day, and take in the distant gunfire. Every night, there were gunshots, and we always tried to figure out what kind of weapon it was. "It is nine millimeters." Typically, a police chase would occur, with police cars speeding through in pursuit of a man driving a stolen vehicle. After that, everyone would return home and have dinner with their loved ones. I would grab my computer, board a minibus, travel home, sleep, and then return the following day to repeat the process.

A year went by. Next, two. I was no closer to having the funds to enroll in school, and I had ceased making plans for it.

The tough part of the hood is that you're always working and you think something is happening, but in reality, nothing is happening. Every day from seven in the morning until seven at night, I was out there asking: How can we make ten rand into twenty? In what way can we make twenty into fifty? How do I make fifty become one hundred? We would spend it on food and possibly some beer at the end of the day, and when we returned home, the question was: How can we make ten into twenty? In what way can we make twenty into fifty? Flipping that money took an entire day of work. You had to be moving, thinking, and walking. You needed to find a guy, meet a guy, and get to a guy. Even though we would frequently finish up at zero, I always felt like I had accomplished a lot.

To work is to hustle, just as Internet browsing is to read. Even though you haven't read a book in a year, the amount of material you consume online over the course of a year—including lists, Facebook posts, and tweets—is equal to a tonne of books. In retrospect, that's what hustling was. It's maximum work for little reward. The wheel is a hamster. I would have obtained an MBA if I had dedicated all that effort to my studies. I chose to major in hustle instead, which no university would award me a degree for.

The power and thrill of Alex first drew me in, but more significantly, I felt more accepted there than I had in high school or any other place. A few folks arched an eyebrow at me when I first arrived. "Who is this kid of color?" However, the hood is not judgmental. You can be there if you so choose. Although I was officially an outsider in the neighborhood because I didn't live there, I didn't feel like one for the first time in my life.

Additionally, the hood is a relaxing, low-stress lifestyle. You don't have to ask yourself the big questions since all of your mental energy is focused on getting by. Who am I? What am I meant to be? Am I doing enough? In the neighborhood, it's OK for a forty-year-old man to live in your mother's home and solicit money from strangers. In the neighborhood, you never feel inadequate because there is always someone worse off than you, and you don't feel the need to put in more effort because the greatest success isn't all that much better than you either. You can live in suspended animation thanks to it.

There's also a great sense of community in the area. From the crackhead to the police officer, everyone knows everyone. People look out for each other. In the neighborhood, if your mother asks you to do something, you must comply. They said, "Can I send you?" You seem to be everyone's child and everyone is your mother.

"May I send you?"

"Yes, what do you need?"

"Go buy bread and milk for me."

"That's cool, yeah."

After she gives you some cash, you go buy bread and milk. You don't say no as long as it doesn't cost you anything and you're not too busy.

Sharing is the most important thing in the hood. You cannot become wealthy by yourself. Do you have any money? Why don't you assist others? Everyone pitches in to aid the elderly woman on the block. You purchase beer for each and every person. You disperse it. Everyone needs to understand how their success helps the community, or else they will target you.

The township also enforces its own laws. The municipality deals with those who are detected stealing. The township handles with those who are detected breaking into homes. I hope the cops catch you before the township does if you are found raping a woman. People avoid getting involved when a lady is being beaten. The number of inquiries with a beating is excessive. Why are they fighting? Who is in charge? Who initiated it? Rape, however, is rape. Stealing is theft. The community has been desecrated by you.

Comfort can be treacherous, but the hood was oddly cozy. Comfort offers both a floor and a ceiling. Like the rest of us in our gang, our guy G was unemployed and just hanging out. He then found employment at a posh clothes boutique. He would go to work every morning, and the boys would make fun of him for doing so. Everyone would laugh at him when we saw him going out suited up. "Look at you in your nice clothes, G!" "Oh, G, are you going to see the white man today?" "Remember to bring some books back from the library, G!"

We were hanging out on the wall one morning after G had been working there for a month when he emerged wearing his socks and slippers. He wasn't wearing business attire.

"Hey, G, what's happening? What's going on at work?

"Oh, I no longer work there."

"Why?"

"I was fired after they accused me of stealing something."

And I'll always remember thinking that it seemed like he did it intentionally. In an attempt to regain acceptance into the gang, he ruined himself.

There is a pull from the hood. It never lets you go, but it also never abandons you. Because you are disrespecting the place that created you, raised you, and never turned you away by choosing to leave. And that location retaliates.

It's time to leave as soon as things in the neighborhood start to go your way. because you will be pulled back in by the hood. It'll figure something out. Something will be found by the police after a person steals something and puts it in your automobile. You must leave. You believe you can. You'll start to feel better and you'll take your friends from your neighborhood out to a great club, but before you know it, someone causes a fight, one of your pals pulls a gun, someone is shot, and you're left wondering, "What just happened?"

The hood occurred.

One evening, I was DJing a party in Lombardy East, a wealthier, middle-class black community, just outside of Alex. The noise prompted a call to the police. They rushed in brandishing machine weapons and riot gear. That's the way our police operate. We don't have huge and small. Americans simply refer to our regular police as SWAT. They came to find out where the music was coming from, and I was the source. One police officer approached me as I was using my computer and pulled out a huge assault gun.

"You need to stop this immediately."

"All right," I said. "I'm going to shut it down."

However, I have Windows 95 installed. It took ages for Windows 95 to shut down. I was shutting down programs and windows. I didn't want to turn off the power and risk damaging my fat Seagate drive, which was prone to damage. It's obvious that none of that mattered to this cop.

"Stop it! Stop it!

"I am! I'm going to shut it down! I must shut down the programs.

The cop was growing anxious, and the crowd was growing irate. He shot the computer and moved his rifle away from me. However, he shot the monitor, demonstrating his obvious lack of computer knowledge. The song continued to play even after the monitor burst. With music playing and everyone running and in a panic due to the gunshot, there was now anarchy. To turn it off, I pulled the power line from the tower. The police then began sprinkling the gathering with tear gas.

Neither the music nor I had anything to do with the tear gas. The police just use tear gas to put an end to gatherings in black communities, much like when a bar turns on the lights to warn everyone to leave.

I misplaced the hard drive. The monitor was apparently fried by the explosion, despite the fact that the police officer had shot it. Although it was unable to read the drive, the machine would still start up. I had lost my music collection. It had taken me years to gather the music collection, even if I had the funds for a new hard disk. It could not be replaced. The business of DJing was over. The sale of CDs was completed. Suddenly, our crew's primary source of income was gone. All we could do was hustle, and we hustled even harder, trying to double the little money we had on hand by purchasing this in order to flip it for that. We began depleting our money, and within a month, we were barely making ends meet.

Then, one evening after work, the black Mr. Burns, our acquaintance from the airport, stopped by.

He exclaimed, "Hey, look what I found."

"What do you have?"

"A camera."

That camera will always be in my memory. The camera was digital. I took it and switched it on after we purchased it from him. I felt like shit when I saw all the images of a gorgeous white family on vacation. I had never given any thought to the other items we had purchased. Electric razors, electric toothbrushes, and Nikes. Who gives a damn? Yes, the supermarket's missing pallet of Corn Flakes could lead to someone losing their job, but that's a long way off. You don't give it much thought. This camera, however, had a face. Knowing how much my family photos meant to me, I looked through them and concluded that I hadn't stolen a camera. Someone's memories have been taken by me. Someone's life has been taken by me.

It's really odd, because during my two years of working hard, I never once considered it a crime. Sincerely, I didn't think it was awful. It's just items that folks discovered. White individuals are insured. Whatever the justification, it was useful. We in society treat each other horribly because we are blind to the person we are harming. Their face is hidden from us. They are not considered human by us. In order to keep the victims of apartheid out of sight and out of mind, the hood was constructed in the first place. Because white people would realize that slavery is unacceptable if they ever saw black people as human. Because we don't live with other people, we exist in a world where we are blind to the consequences of our actions. If an investment banker had to live alongside the individuals he was defrauding of their subprime mortgages, it would be far more difficult for him to do so. It would never be worthwhile for us to commit the crimes in the first place if we could sympathize with one another and see each other's suffering.

I never sold the camera, even though we desperately needed the money. I couldn't do it because I felt too horrible about it, thinking it would be bad karma. I know it seems silly, and it didn't bring the family their camera back. That camera forced me to face the reality that what I was doing was terrible and that there were people on the other end of it.

Our group was invited to compete against another crew in a dance in Soweto one evening. Hector, their best dancer and one of the top dancers in South Africa at the time, was scheduled to compete against Hitler. This was a really important invitation. We were heading over there to represent our neighborhood. Soweto and Alex have always been bitter rivals. Alexandra was perceived as the gritty and filthy township, whereas Soweto was perceived as the aristocratic township. Hector was from the affluent, pleasant area of Soweto known as Diepkloof. Following democracy, the first million-rand homes were constructed in Diepkloof. Hey, we are no longer a township. We are currently constructing lovely stuff. That was the mindset. We faced off against them. Hitler spent an entire week practicing.

On the night of the dance, Hitler, Mzi, Bheki, and G, as well as Bongani, rode in a minibus to Diepkloof. The competition was won by Hector. Everything went down after G was seen kissing one of their girls, which led to a confrontation. Around one in the morning, as we were leaving Diepkloof to enter the freeway on our trip back to Alex, several police stopped our minibus. They searched it after forcing everyone to exit. When one of the policemen returned, we were outside, lined up next to the car.

He declared, "We've found a gun." "Whose firearm is it?"

Each of us shrugged.

We said, "We're not sure."

"Nope, someone is aware. It belongs to someone.

Bongani remarked, "Officer, we really don't know."

He gave Bongani a forceful slap across the face.

"You're lying to me!"

He then proceeded to hit each of us across the face while reprimanding us for the gun. All we could do was accept it while standing there.

The policeman remarked, "You guys are trash." "Where are you from?"

"Alex."

"Oh, all right, I see. Alex's dogs. You come here and rape women, rob people, and take over cars. A group of fucking idiots.

"No, we're dancers. We're not sure—

"I'm not interested. You will all be imprisoned until we identify the owner of this firearm.

We eventually understood what was happening. We were being shaken down for a bribe by this cop. Everyone uses the term "spot fine." You and the police officer perform a complex dance in which you express the thing without actually saying it.

"Is there anything we can do?" you ask the officer.

"What are you expecting me to do?"

We sincerely apologize, Officer. What are our options?

"You tell me."

After that, you are expected to fabricate a scenario in which you tell the police officer how much cash you are carrying. which we were unable to accomplish due to a lack of funds. Thus, he led us to the prison. The bus was a public one. Although anyone could have had the gun, only the Alex guys were taken into custody. The rest of the car was free to leave. We were led to the police station, where we were placed in a cell and taken out one by one to be questioned by the officers. I had to provide my home location, Highlands North, when they drew me aside. I got the most perplexed face from the cop.

He remarked, "You're not from Alex." "Why are you interacting with these criminals?" I was at a loss for words. He gave me a fierce gaze. "Hear me out, wealthy boy. Do you find running around with these men enjoyable? This is no longer play-play. I'll let you go if you just tell me the truth about your friends and the gun.

He tossed me back in the jail when I told him no. We stayed overnight, and when I called a friend the following day, he claimed he could borrow the cash from his father to get us out. The father came down later that day and made the payment. Although it was a bribe, the police insisted on calling it "bail." Formally, we were never taken into custody or processed. No paperwork was present.

It shook us, but after we went out, everything was alright. We were out on the streets every day, working hard and seeming to be part of the gangs, but in reality, we were always more cheese than hood. In order to survive in the world we were living in, we had developed this self-concept. Because of their origins and appearance, Bongani and the other East Bank men just had very little hope. In that case, you have two possibilities. If you're among the fortunate few who even receive that much, you accept the retail position and flip hamburgers at McDonald's. The alternative is to put on this façade and get tougher. Because you are unable to leave the hood, you must abide by its laws in order to survive.

Although I wasn't from that world, I made the decision to live there. I was, if anything, a fake. I was just as involved in it on a daily basis as everyone else, but I kept in the back of my mind that I had other choices. I could go. They were unable to.

Chapter 17: The World Doesn't Love You

I never got a single inch from my mother. Every time I got into trouble, I had to endure lectures, discipline, hidings, and tough love. Each and every time. for each violation. That's what many black parents are like. Before the system acts, they are attempting to discipline you. "This must be done to you before the police do it." Since the day you are old enough to venture out onto the street, where the law is waiting, it is all that black parents consider.

Being arrested was just part of Alex's existence. It was so widespread that we developed a shorthand sign for it out on the corner that clapped your wrists together as if you were being placed in handcuffs. Everyone understood what that meant.
"Where is Bongani?"
Clap your hands together.
"Oh, sh*t. When?
"Friday evening."
"Gosh."
Mom detested the hood. There, she didn't like my pals. She didn't even want them to enter the house if I brought them back. She would say, "I don't like those boys." She detested what they stood for, not

them specifically. She would say, "You and those boys get into so much shit." "Your surroundings can shape who you are, so you need to be mindful of who you surround yourself with."

She claimed that the fact that the hood didn't put any pressure on me to improve was what she detested most about it. She wanted me to visit my cousin at his university and spend time with him.

"What makes being in the neighborhood or at university different?" I would say. "It's not as though I'm attending college."

Yes, but you will succumb to the pressures of college. You are someone I know. You won't stand by and let these guys surpass you. You will also become positive and progressive if you are in a good and progressive environment. You refuse to modify your life despite my repeated requests. Don't call me when you get arrested because you will one day. To give you a lesson, I'll order the cops to put you in jail.

Because some black parents would truly practice the greatest form of tough love by refusing to pay their child's bail or hire a lawyer. However, it doesn't always work since you're offering the child harsh criticism when, in reality, he may just need affection. The remainder of his life will be the lesson you're attempting to teach him.

I spotted an advertisement in the paper one morning. There was a mobile phone clearance sale going on, and the prices were so outrageous that I knew Bongani and I could sell them for a profit. Too far to walk and too remote to take a minibus, this store was located in the suburbs. Luckily, our backyard included a number of vintage cars and my stepfather's workshop.

Since I was fourteen, I had been using Abel's junkers as a means of transportation. I would say that I was testing them to ensure that the repairs were done appropriately. That didn't seem amusing to Abel. I had been caught numerous times, caught, and punished by my mother. However, I had never let that deter me from taking action.

The majority of these junkers weren't allowed on the streets. Neither their number plates nor their registrations were correct. Fortunately, Abel had a stack of vintage license plates at the garage's rear. I soon discovered that I could simply install one on an outdated vehicle and drive. I wasn't considering any of the consequences of this when I was nineteen or possibly twenty. When no one else was around, I went to Abel's garage, grabbed the red Mazda I had driven to the matric dance, put some old license plates on it, and went looking for cheap cell phones.

In Hillbrow, I was pulled over. When South African police pull you over, they don't offer you a reason. Simply put, police officers pull you over because they are law enforcement officials and have the authority to do so. Police would pull individuals over and say things like, "You didn't signal," or "Your taillight's out," in American movies I used to watch. Why American police officers bother lying is a question I've always had. I like that South Africa hasn't perfected the system to the point that we feel compelled to tell lies.
"Are you aware of the reason I stopped you?"
"Because I'm Black and you're a police officer?"
That's right. Please provide a license and registration.
One of those times when I wanted to yell, "Hey, I know you guys are racially profiling me!" was when the policeman pulled me over. However, I was breaking the law at the time, so I was unable to argue the case. The policeman approached my window and asked me the usual questions. Where are you heading? Is this your vehicle? Whose vehicle is this? I was unable to respond. I froze totally.

Ironically, as a young person, I was more concerned about getting into problems with my parents than the law. I'd had encounters with the police in Alexandra and Soweto, but it was usually more about the situation: a minibus raid, a party being shut down. Although the law was all around me, Trevor in particular had never been subject to it. Additionally, the law seems reasonable to someone who has little experience with it—cops are generally dicks, but you also understand that they have a job to do.

Conversely, your parents are completely irrational. It feels like they condemn you to life in prison for each offense, and they have been your judge, juror, and executioner throughout your entire youth. When I should have been afraid of the police officer, all I could think was, "Sh*t shit shit," and "I'm going to get into a lot of trouble when I get home."

When the police called in the license plate registration, they found that it did not match the vehicle. He was really after me now. "Your name is not on this car! Why are these plates acting this way? Get out of the car! Only then did it occur to me: Ohhhhh, shit. I'm in serious trouble now. He placed me in handcuffs as soon as I got out of the car and informed me that I was being detained on suspicion of operating a stolen vehicle. The automobile was seized, and he took me in.

In terms of appearance, the Hillbrow police station is identical to all other South African police stations. Separate nodes in a police state's central nervous system, they were all constructed by the same contractor during the height of apartheid. You most likely wouldn't even be aware that you had moved if you were blindfolded and carried from one place to another. Like a hospital, they are institutional, hygienic, and have inexpensive floor tiles and fluorescent lighting. After escorting me inside, my officer seated me at the front desk for reservations. I was fingerprinted and charged.

They had been inspecting the automobile in the interim, which wasn't going well for me either. I believed I would avoid difficulties if I took the junkers instead of a legitimate client's automobile whenever I borrowed one from Abel's workshop. It was an error. Since the Mazda was one of Abel's junkers, its ownership was unclear. The situation would have been resolved if the owner had been contacted by the police, who would have informed them that the vehicle had been taken in for repairs. I was unable to establish I hadn't stolen the car because it had no owner.

At the period, carjackings were also frequent in South Africa. They were so frequent that you weren't even shocked when they occurred. You would receive a call just as a friend was about to arrive for a dinner party.

I apologize. was carjacked. I will be late.
"Oh, that's awful. Hello everyone! Dave was carjacked.
"I'm sorry, Dave!"
And the celebration would go on. If the victim of the carjacking survives, that is. They frequently didn't. People were constantly being

shot for their vehicles. I couldn't prove that I hadn't stolen the car, but I also couldn't prove that I hadn't killed someone for it. I was being grilled by the police. "Boy, you slaughter people to obtain that car? Well? Are you a murderer?

I was very, really in trouble. My parents were my only source of support. It would have all been resolved with a single call. My stepfather is this person. He works as a mechanic. I shouldn't have borrowed his automobile. Completed. In the worst case scenario, I would receive a smack on the wrist for operating an unregistered vehicle. What would I receive at home, though?

Arrested on suspicion of auto theft and a likely suspect in carjacking or murder, I sat in the police station and contemplated if I should call my parents or go to jail. It crossed my mind that my stepfather might kill me. That was a completely plausible scenario in my mind. I was thinking that my mother would make things worse. I don't currently want her as a character witness. She refuses to assist me. since she had promised not to. "Don't call me if you ever get arrested." I didn't think she was the kind of person I needed who could relate to my situation. I didn't call my parents, therefore. I concluded that I didn't require them. I was a man. I could do it by myself. I called my cousin and instructed him to keep the incident a secret until I decided what to do. Now I simply needed to decide what to do.
It was almost lights-out when I was processed because I had been picked up late in the afternoon. Whether I liked it or not, I was spending the night in jail. A police officer then drew me aside and explained what I was getting into.

In South Africa, the process include being arrested and detained in a police station cell until your bail hearing. After reviewing your case and hearing arguments from both sides, the judge decides whether to dismiss the charges or set bail and a trial date. You pay and return home if you are able to post bail. However, there are numerous ways that your bail hearing could go awry: You are assigned a counsel by the court who has not read your case and is unaware of the facts. Your bail cannot be paid by your relatives. It's even possible that the court is backing up. We apologize, but we're too busy. Hearings are over for today. The cause is irrelevant. You cannot return to jail once you are released from there. You go to prison to await trial if your case isn't settled that day. Even the awaiting-trial area of the prison is quite hazardous since it houses people who have been picked up for everything from traffic infractions to serious, hardened criminals. In prison, you are housed alongside those who are awaiting trial, not the general public. Together, you are stranded there for days, weeks, or perhaps months. In America, it is the same. You can fall through the cracks if you're poor and don't understand how the system operates. Then, you'll find yourself in a strange limbo where you're not in jail but you're also not out of jail. You are still imprisoned and unable to leave even though you have not been found guilty of any crimes.

You don't want to attend your bond hearing, this officer said, pulling me aside. They will assign you a state attorney who is unaware of the situation. There won't be any time for you. After he requests a postponement from the judge, you may or may not be released. You don't want to do that, I assure you. You are free to remain here for however long you choose. Before you approach a court or a judge, you should consult with an attorney to prepare yourself. He wasn't being altruistic when he gave me this counsel. In exchange for a kickback, he established an agreement with a defense lawyer that sent him clients. I called the lawyer he gave me his business card, and he agreed to take on my case. He instructed me to remain motionless while he took care of everything.

Despite their kindness, lawyers don't work for free, thus I needed money now. I asked a friend over the phone if he could approach his father for a loan. He promised to take care of it. After speaking with his father, the lawyer received his retainer the following day.

I thought I had things under control now that the lawyer was taken care of. It made me feel very sticky. Most importantly, Mom and Abel were unaware that I had addressed the matter.

A police officer arrived and took my belongings when it was time to turn down the lights. My shoelaces, my wallet, and my belt.

"Why are my shoelaces necessary for you?"

"To avoid hanging yourself."

"All right."

The seriousness of my predicament hadn't yet set me when he stated it. I thought, "This is no big deal," as I made my way to the station's holding cell and saw the other six men inside. Everything will be awesome. I will get out of this situation. That's what I believed until the guard barked, "Lights out!" and the cell door clanged shut behind me. I thought, "Oh, shit," at that point. This is true.

I was handed a scratchy blanket and a mat by the guards. I tried to settle in after rolling them out on the concrete floor. My mind was reeling from every awful prison film I had ever seen. I was afraid I would be raped. Someone is going to rape me. Someone is going to rape me. Naturally, though, I was not raped because this was not a prison. As I would soon learn, there is a significant difference—it was jail.

I had the brief feeling that everything was a dream as I woke up the following morning. Then I remembered that it wasn't as I glanced around. When breakfast arrived, I took a seat and waited.

The majority of a day in jail is spent in stillness, broken only by guards yelling obscenities at you when they do roll call. No one speaks inside the holding cell. No one enters a prison cell and greets the inmates. My name is Brian. Because nobody wants to look weak and everyone is scared. Not a single person wants to be the bitch. Nobody desires to be the one slain. I attempted to act like the clichés of what I thought people in prison would do because I didn't want anyone to know that I was only a youngster jailed for a traffic infraction.

Everyone in South Africa is aware that the most vicious and barbaric gangsters are those of color. You've been exposed to this stereotype your entire life. The Numbers Gangs—the 26s, 27s, and 28s—are the most well-known colors gangs. The prisons are under their jurisdiction. Like Mexican drug cartels, they are notorious for their savagery and brutality—maiming, torturing, raping, and chopping off people's heads—not to make money but simply to demonstrate their ruthlessness and savagery. Many of these groups actually take inspiration from the Mexican gangs. The Converse All Stars with the Dickies slacks and the open shirt that is only buttoned at the top appear alike.

By the time I was a teenager, police officers and security personnel would typically profile me based on my appearance rather than my race. I once accompanied my cousin and his friend to a club. After searching Mlungisi, the bouncer waved him inside. He waved our guy in after searching him. He then got up in my face and looked me over.
"Where is your blade?"
"I have no knife with me."
You have a knife somewhere, I'm sure of it. "Where is it?"
He looked me over as if I were trouble, and after a long search, he gave up and let me in.
"Don't be a jerk! Alright?
I reasoned that if I was incarcerated, people would assume I was a violent criminal, the type of person of color who ends up in jail. I therefore exaggerated it. I played the stereotype; I took on this persona. I began speaking in broken Afrikaans with a thick colored accent whenever the police asked me a question. Imagine a white man in America who is just dark enough to seem Latino, strutting about a prison, acting out cheesy movie dialogue about Mexican gangsters. "Ese, things are going to get crazy." I was essentially performing the South African equivalent of it. This was my clever prison survival strategy. However, it was successful. The men in the cell with me were there for petty theft, domestic violence, and drunk driving. They were ignorant of the characteristics of actual colored gangsters. I was left alone by everyone.

No one was aware that we were all participating in a game. Everyone was staring at me like, "I'm dangerous," when I walked in that first night. Please don't mess with me. "Shit, these people are seasoned criminals," I said. I am not a criminal, so I shouldn't be here. The following day, however, things swiftly changed. I continued to wait for my lawyer, fresh individuals began to arrive, and one by one, the guys went off to their hearings. I was the seasoned man now, performing my colored-gangster routine and giving the new guys the same "I'm dangerous" expression. Please don't mess with me. They said, "Shit, he's a hardened criminal," after glancing at me. Since I am not like him, I shouldn't be here. We continued to go round and round.

It seemed to me at one point that everyone in that cell might be pretending. Picked up for unpaid parking tickets and other violations, we were all good guys from excellent families and lovely communities. We might have been enjoying ourselves immensely while eating together, playing cards, and discussing ladies and soccer. However, it didn't occur because everyone had assumed this risky stance and no one spoke because they were all terrified of the identities the other guys were assuming. "Oh, honey, that was rough," the men would say as they left and returned home to their families. In there were some actual crooks. One man of color was there. He was a killer, man.

I was fine after I figured out the game. I calmed down. I was thinking again, I understood. This is not a major issue. In fact, the food was good. They served you these peanut butter sandwiches on big bread slices for breakfast. Rice and chicken for lunch. Although it contained more water than tea and was excessively hot, the tea was nonetheless palatable. The task assigned to the older, difficult-to-release inmates was to clean the cells and distribute periodicals for your perusal. It was quite soothing.

 I recall thinking to myself, "This isn't so bad," while I was eating a dinner. I spend a lot of time with men. There are no household tasks. No expenses to cover. No one who is always bugging me and giving me instructions. Sandwiches with peanut butter? I always eat peanut butter sandwiches, shit. This is quite lovely. This is something I could do. I honestly thought about going to jail because I was so terrified of the ass-whooping that was waiting for me at home. I briefly believed that I had a plan. "I'll disappear for a few years, return, and claim that I was abducted; my mother won't find out and will only be pleased to see me."

The biggest man I had ever seen was hauled in by the police on the third day. This man was enormous. enormous muscles. dark complexion. a hardened face. He seems capable of killing us all. The moment he entered, the tough-guy routines that the other inmates and I had been using against each other ended. Everyone was afraid. All of us gazed at him. "Oh, screw it."
 When the police took him up, this man was, for whatever reason, half-naked. He was dressed in a ripped wifebeater that was much too small

and short pants that resembled capris that the police had scrounged together for him at the station. He had the appearance of the Incredible Hulk in black.

This man went to the corner and sat by himself. No one spoke. Everyone anxiously watched and awaited his next move. Then one of the officers returned and summoned the Hulk because they wanted his knowledge. The officer began to question him, but the man repeatedly shook his head and said he didn't understand. The policeman spoke Zulu. Tsonga was being spoken by the Hulk. Black person to Black person—the Tower of Babel—and none could comprehend the other. Since my stepfather was Tsonga, I had picked up the language along the road, even though not many people in South Africa spoke it. I stepped in and translated for the police officer and the other man after overhearing them arguing back and forth without anything being understood.

"If you speak to a man in a language he understands, that goes to his head," Nelson Mandela famously remarked. Speaking to him in his own tongue will win his heart. He was absolutely correct. You're telling someone, "I know that you have a culture and identity that exists beyond me," when you try to speak their language, even if it's just a few simple words here and there. You seem like a human to me.

The Hulk experienced precisely that. This face, which had appeared so cruel and menacing, filled up with gratitude the moment I talked to him. "Oh, na khensa, na khensa, na khensa." Hello, Wena Mani. Are you xitiela kwini xiTsonga, mufana wa mukhaladi? "U huma kwini?" Oh, I am really grateful. Thank you so much. Who are you? How is Tsonga known to a man of color? From where do you hail?

I knew he wasn't the Hulk after we had a conversation. He was the world's largest teddy bear, the loveliest man, and a kind giant. He was uneducated and basic. It wasn't at all what I had thought he was up to—murder, squeezing a family to death with his bare hands. He had been taken into custody for stealing PlayStation games. When he saw how much these games went for, he figured he could steal a couple and sell them to white kids and make a lot of money. He was unemployed and needed the money to send home to his family. I knew he wasn't some seasoned crook as soon as he said that. I am familiar with the world of pirated content; stolen video games are worthless as it is less expensive and dangerous to replicate them, like Bolo's parents did.

I did my best to assist him. He also waited in the cell, waiting for me to explain my strategy of postponing your bail hearing until you have a solid case. We clicked and spent a few days together, enjoying ourselves and getting to know one another. We were the vicious colored mobster and his ominous, Hulk-like companion, and nobody else in the jail knew what to think of us. I was all too familiar with the South African story he told me: The man, who is a member of what is effectively a slave labor force, works on a farm while growing up during apartheid. At least it's something, even though it's a living hell. He receives a meager salary, but at least he gets paid. Throughout the day, he is instructed on where to go and what to do. After apartheid ends, he no longer even has that. He travels to Johannesburg in search of employment while attempting to provide for his family back home. He's lost, though. He is uneducated. He lacks any abilities. He is unsure of where to go and what to do. Although he has been taught that the world fears him, the truth is that he fears the world because he lacks the resources to deal with it. What does he do, then? He is a jerk. He turns becomes a small-time burglar. He goes and goes from prison. A few days later, he's at a store and he sees some PlayStation games and he takes them, but he doesn't even know enough to realize that he's stolen something worthless. He gets lucky and finds some construction work, but he gets laid off from that.

I was sorry for him. The longer I was incarcerated, the more I understood that the law is completely irrational. It's a lottery. What hue is your skin? How much cash do you possess? Who is your attorney? Who is the arbiter? Driving with a bad license plate was a more serious offense than stealing PlayStation games. Although he had broken the law, he was no more of a criminal than I was. The distinction was that he had no family or friends to support him. The only thing he could afford was a state lawyer. Everyone in the courtroom was going to assume the worst about him when he stood in the dock unable to speak or understand English. He would spend some time in prison before being released with the same nothing he had before. I would estimate that he was between thirty-five and forty years old, and he was looking forward to another thirty-five to forty years of the same.

My hearing day arrived. I bid my new friend farewell and sent him my best wishes. I was then taken to the courthouse to face my fate while handcuffed and placed in the rear of a police van. The holding cell where you await your hearing in South African courts is a huge pen beneath the courtroom; instead of being escorted through the hallways, you must ascend a flight of steps to enter the dock. This is done to reduce your exposure and your chances of escaping. In the holding cell, you are placed with inmates who have been detained for weeks or months pending trial. From white-collar crooks to men apprehended at traffic stops to actual, hard-core criminals with tattoos from jail, it's a strange mix. A miserable hive of filth and villainy, it's similar to the Star Wars cantina scene where the band is playing music, Han Solo is in the corner, and all the villains and bounty hunters from throughout the universe are gathered. The only difference is that there is no music and no Han Solo.

Although my time with these individuals was brief, I was able to observe the distinction between jail and prison at that very moment. I observed the distinction between those who have committed crimes and those who are criminals. I could see how hard people's faces were. I reflected on how foolish I had been only a few hours earlier, believing that I could manage incarceration and that it wasn't that horrible. Now I genuinely feared what would befall me.

I was a young man with smooth skin and a fresh face when I entered that holding pen. I had a huge Afro at the time, and the only way to manage it was to wear it in a pretty ponytail. I resembled Maxwell. After the soldiers shut the door behind me, this eerie elderly man shouted in Zulu from the rear, "Ha, ha, ha! Madoda he! Indoda enhle kangaka angikaze ngibone! Obuhle sizoba nobusuku! "Yo, yo, yo! Guys, damn you. This is the most beautiful man I have ever seen. Tonight is going to be a great night!
Fuuuuuuuuck.

As I entered, I saw a young man crying uncontrollably and having a full breakdown next to me. He was talking to himself. I suppose he believed I looked like a kindred person he could chat to because he looked up and met my eyes. He approached me directly and began sobbing as he told me how the gangs had raped and beaten him daily, taken his clothes and shoes, and arrested and imprisoned him. He wasn't a gangster. He was intelligent and articulate. He wanted to commit suicide since he had been waiting a year for his case to be heard. I was terrified of God because of that guy.

I surveyed the detention cell. There were probably a hundred men in there, all of them dispersed and huddled into their distinct racial groups: a few white men off to one side, a couple of Indians off to themselves, a bunch of black people in one corner, and colored people in another. As soon as we entered the police van, the people who had been with me immediately left to join the groups to which they belonged. I went cold.

I was unsure of where to go.

I turned to face the colorful corner. I was looking into South Africa's most vicious and infamous prison gang. Despite my appearance, I wasn't them. They would find out I was a phony if I went over there acting like a gangster. No, no, no. My friend, that game was done. Having colored gangsters against me was the last thing I needed.

What if I went to the black corner, though? Would the black males understand why I was approaching them if I were not a black person, even if I am aware that I am and identify as black? And why would I go there in the first place? For the colored gangs, going to the colored corner as a phony colored person can aggravate them even more than going to the black corner as a perceived colored person. Because I had experienced that throughout my life. When they saw me interacting with Black folks, individuals of color would approach me and want to fight. In the holding cell, I envisioned myself inciting a racial conflict.

"Hey! Why do you spend time with Black people?

"Because my race is Black."

"No, you're not. You're a person of color.

Yes, indeed. I see how that appears, friend, but allow me to clarify. Actually, it's a funny story. Since race is a societal construct since my mother is Black and my father is White,

That was not going to be effective. Not in this place.

All of this happened quickly and spontaneously in my mind. I was looking at people, scanning the room, calculating crazily, and evaluating the factors. This will happen if I come here. That's if I go there. Every time and everywhere I ever had to be a chameleon, move between groups, or explain who I was, my entire life was flashing before me—the school playground, the Soweto spaza stores, the streets of Eden Park. It was similar to the high school cafeteria, but it was the high school cafeteria from hell since I could be raped, stabbed, or beaten if I chose the incorrect table. Never in my life had I been so afraid. I still had to choose, though. Because you have to choose a side because racism exists. You may claim that you are impartial, but you will eventually have to choose a side in life.

I chose white that day. They simply didn't seem capable of harming me. The group consisted of a few middle-aged, ordinary white men. I approached them. We spent some time together and talked. They were primarily involved in money-schemes, fraud, racketeering, and white-collar crimes. If someone came over trying to cause trouble, they would be useless because they would also get kicked in the ass. However, they had no intention of harming me. I was secure.

Fortunately, the time passed quite rapidly. I was only there for an hour before I was summoned to court, where a judge would decide whether to release me or put me in jail while I awaited trial. One of the white males approached me as I was walking away. "Be careful not to return down here," he urged. "Weep in front of the judge; take any necessary action. Your life will never be the same if you go up and are sent back down here.

I discovered my attorney waiting up in the courtroom. In the gallery, my cousin Mlungisi was also present and prepared to deposit my bail should the situation work out.
The judge glanced up at me as the bailiff recited my case number.
He asked, "How are you?"
I lost it. After almost a week of maintaining this tough-guy persona, I simply couldn't keep it up any longer.
"Your Honor, I'm not okay. I'm not doing well.
He appeared perplexed. "What?"

"I'm not fine, sir," I responded. I'm in a lot of pain.

"Why are you stating this to me?"

"Because you inquired about my well-being."

"Who made the inquiry?"

"You did. I was just asked.

"I didn't ask how you were doing. 'Who are you?' I asked. Why would I waste time inquiring about your well-being? This is a prison. Everyone down there is in pain, I know that. We would be here all day if I asked everyone how they were doing. 'Who are you?' I asked. For the record, please state your name.

"Nathan Trevor."

"All right. We can now continue.

When the entire courtroom burst out laughing, I followed suit. Now that I was laughing, though, I was even more terrified since I didn't want the judge to think I wasn't paying attention.

As it happened, I didn't have to worry. The next few minutes were all that was needed. The prosecution had spoken with my lawyer, and everything had been planned in advance. He made my argument. I didn't have any priors. I posed no threat. The other side did not raise any objections. After setting my bond and assigning my trial date, the judge let me leave.

When the sunlight kissed my face as I was leaving the court, I exclaimed, "Sweetheart Jesus, I will never return there again." A week in jail is a long, long time, even if it had only been a week and the food wasn't too horrible and the cell wasn't particularly unpleasant. Without shoelaces for a week is a very long time. A week without sun or clocks can seem like an eternity. I couldn't even begin to conceive the possibility of something worse, the idea of working in a genuine prison.

Mlungisi and I drove to his house, where I showered and slept. He returned me to my mother's place the following day. I pretended to be very casual as I walked up the driveway. I was going to claim that I had been staying with Mlungisi for a few days. I entered the house as if nothing had occurred. "Hi, Mom! What's going on? Mom didn't ask me any questions or say anything. "Okay," I said. Cool. We're doing fine.

I spent the majority of the day there. We were conversing at the kitchen table later in the day. My mom gave me this look and shook her head slowly as I continued to tell her all the stories of what Mlungisi and I had been doing that week. I had never seen her give a look like that before. "One day, I'm going to catch you" wasn't it. It wasn't condemnation or rage. It was a letdown. She was wounded. "What?" "I said." "What is it?"

"Boy, who do you think paid your bail?" she asked. What? Who do you believe covered your attorney's fees? Do you believe I'm a fool? Did you really believe that nobody would inform me?

The truth was revealed. She had known, of course: the automobile. All along, it had been absent. The red Mazda that was missing from the driveway was the proof of my crime, but I had been too preoccupied with dealing with incarceration and hiding my tracks to notice it. Naturally, after I called my friend and he requested his father for the money for the lawyer, the father questioned him about the purpose of the money and, as a parent himself, called my mother right away. She had provided my pal with the funds to cover the attorney's fees. She had provided my cousin with the funds to cover my bail. I thought I was so slick during the entire week I was in jail. However, she had been aware of everything the entire time.

She remarked, "You forget that I ride you so hard and give you so much shit because I love you. I know you see me as some crazy old bitch nagging at you." I have always acted out of love in all I have done. The world will punish you even more severely if I don't. You are not loved by the world. The police don't love you if they catch you. I'm attempting to save you when I beat you. They are attempting to murder you when they beat you.

Chapter 18: My Mother's Life

For the first time, I began to attract the attention of girls after getting my hair cornrowed for the matric dance. In fact, I went on dates. There were instances when I believed it was because I looked better. At other times, I believed it was because girls found it attractive that I was enduring the same amount of suffering as they were in order to be attractive. In any case, I was determined not to alter the recipe once I achieved success. I continued to return to the salon once a week, where I would spend hours getting my hair cornrowed and straightened. Just rolling her eyes, my mother would do. She would remark, "I could never date a man who spends more time on his hair than I do."

My mother, dressed as a homeless person, worked in her office Monday through Saturday and lounged in her garden. She would then style her hair, put on a lovely outfit, and accessorize with high shoes for church on Sunday morning, looking stunning. She couldn't help but tease me after getting all dolled up, using the same verbal insults we often exchanged.

"Now, who in the family is the most attractive, huh? The queen is back, darling, so I hope you had a great week being the gorgeous one. To appear like that, you went to the salon for four hours. Just now, I showered.

No son likes to talk about how attractive his mother is, so she was just enjoying herself with me. Because, really, she was gorgeous. Both the exterior and the inside are stunning. I never had the same level of confidence in myself as she did. You could see how pretty she was even when she was working in the garden, covered in muck and wearing overalls.

My father and my stepfather were the only males in my mother's life from the moment I was born, though I can only suppose that she destroyed a lot of hearts in her day. Mighty Mechanics was a garage located in Yeoville, just around the corner from my father's house. My mom would take our Volkswagen there to have it fixed since it kept breaking down. One of the car technicians there, Abel, was a pretty cool guy who we met. When we went to pick up the automobile, I would see him. We spent a lot of time there because the automobile broke down frequently. Even though there was nothing wrong with the car, it finally seemed as though we were there. I was six or seven years old. I didn't fully get what was going on. I was abruptly aware of this man's presence. Tall, lanky, and skinny, he was powerful. He had large hands and long arms. He was able to lift gears and automobile engines. He wasn't attractive, but he was handsome. My mother used to say that there is a certain kind of ugliness that women find appealing, and she appreciated that about him. She referred to him as Abie. Mbuyi, short for Nombuyiselo, was the name he gave her.

I also liked him. Abie had a simple, polite grin and was lovely and funny. He also enjoyed assisting others, particularly those in need. He would pull over to see what he could do if someone's automobile broke down on the freeway. When someone shouted, "Stop, thief!" he was the one who chased after them. Did the elderly woman next door require assistance carrying boxes? That's him. He enjoyed being loved by everyone, which made dealing with his abuse much more difficult. Because you start to believe that you are the evil guy if you believe someone is a monster and everyone else says he is a saint. You can only conclude that I must be to blame for this since you are the only one who is feeling his rage.

I always got along with Abel. He wasn't attempting to be my father, and since my father was still alive, I wasn't searching for a replacement. I thought of him as my mom's cool friend. He began frequenting Eden Park to stay with us. He would occasionally invite us to stay in his Orange Grove garage apartment, which we did. That came to an end when I set fire to the white people's home. We moved into Eden Park together after that.

My mother pulled me aside during a prayer group one evening.

She said, "Hey." "I have something to share with you. We are getting married, Abel and I.

"I don't think that's a good idea," I blurted without even thinking.

I wasn't angry at all. I simply got a gut feeling about the man. Even before the mulberry tree, I had sensed it. My feelings for Abel had not changed as a result of that night; it had merely demonstrated to me his physical prowess.

"I know it's difficult," she remarked. "I know you don't want a new father."

"No," I replied. "That isn't it. Abel appeals to me. I really like him. However, you shouldn't wed him. I probably would have used the word "sinister" if I had known what it was at the time. There's simply something wrong with him. I have no faith in him. He's not a good person, in my opinion.

Although I had always accepted my mom's relationship with this man, I had never given any thought to the prospect of him joining our family as a permanent member. I liked spending time with Abel in the same way that I liked playing with a tiger cub during my first visit to a tiger sanctuary: I liked it, I had fun, but I never considered taking it home.

The truth was always there in front of us, in Abel's name, if there was any question about him. His name was taken directly from the Bible: Abel, the good son and brother. And he fulfilled it, too. Being the eldest, he was obedient, looked after his mother, and looked after his siblings. His family took great delight in him.

However, his English name was Abel. Ngisaveni was his Tsonga name. "Be afraid" is what it implies.

Abel and Mom were married. There was no ring exchange or ceremony. After signing the documents, they left. Andrew, my baby brother, was born about a year later. Although I just dimly recall my mother being gone for a few days and finding this thing in the home that shattered, cried, and got fed when she returned, being nine years older than your sister doesn't really affect you. I was racing about the neighborhood and playing arcade games at the shop instead of changing diapers.

For me, the most significant event surrounding Andrew's birth was our first visit to Abel's family over the Christmas season. They resided in the town of Tzaneen, which was part of Gazankulu, the former apartheid homeland of the Tsonga. The climate of Tzaneen is tropical, hot, and muggy. Mangoes, lychees, and the most exquisite bananas you've ever seen are among the most magnificent fruits grown on the white farms in the area. All of the fruit that we ship to Europe is grown there. However, years of overgrazing and overfarming have destroyed the soil on the black area twenty minutes away. Abel and his younger brother, a police officer, provided for the family, while his mother and his sisters were all conventional stay-at-home mothers. They immediately welcomed us into the family and were all really generous and kind.

I discovered that Tsonga culture is rather patriarchal. We are discussing a society in which women are required to bow when they meet a male. Social connections between men and women are limited. The ladies prepare the food while the men kill the animals. Even the kitchen is off limits to men. When I was nine years old, I found this to be amazing. I was prohibited from doing anything. In Tzaneen, the women wouldn't let my mom do the chores she insisted I do at home, like sweeping the house or washing the dishes.

My mother used to say, "Make your bed, Trevor."

Abel's mother would object, saying, "No, no, no, no." "Trevor needs to go play outside."

While my girl step-cousins had to help the women cook and clean the house, I was forced to run off and have fun. Heaven was where I was.

My mother detested every second of her stay there. This trip was very important to Abel, a firstborn son who was bringing home his own firstborn son. Because the father is away working in the city, the firstborn son in the homelands practically automatically takes on the role of father or husband. The head of the household is the eldest son. He brings up his siblings. As the father's surrogate, his mother shows him some respect. Given that this was Abel's great reunion with Andrew, he anticipated that my mother would also fulfill her custom. However, she declined.

During the day, Tzaneen women worked at several different jobs. In addition to making breakfast, tea, and lunch, they also cleaned and washed. This was really their vacation since the males had been working in the city all year to provide for their families. The women were waiting on them while they were at leisure. After doing whatever macho chores needed to be done, like butchering a goat or whatever, guys would go to a male-only area and hang out and drink while the women cleaned and prepared meals. However, Patricia Noah didn't live in anyone's kitchen, and my mom had been working in the city all year as well. She was a wandering soul. She insisted on traveling to the village on foot, where the men congregated, and conversing with them on an equal footing.

My mother thought it was ridiculous that women were expected to bow to males. She did not, however, decline to do so. She went overboard. It was mocked by her. The other women used this courteous little curtsy while bowing to males. My mother would descend and cower, groveling in the dirt as though she were worshiping a god, and she would remain there for a very long time—long enough to cause great discomfort to everyone. My mother was that. Avoid challenging the system. Make fun of the system. It appeared to Abel that his wife did not value him. Every other man had a submissive rural girl, but now he had this contemporary lady—a Xhosa woman, no less—who was regarded as especially promiscuous and loud-mouthed. My mother refused to return after that first vacation since they were constantly fighting and bickering.

I had grown up in a world dominated by women, but once my mother and Abel were married, and particularly after Andrew was born, I saw him attempt to make his voice heard and force his views on his family. Early on, it was evident that I was not included in such concepts. I served as a reminder that my mother was a person before him. I wasn't even the same hue as his. He, my mother, and the newborn were his family. My mother and I made up my family. In fact, I liked that about him. He never pretended that our connection was anything other than what it was, even though he was my friend at times and not at others. Together, we would laugh and make jokes. Together, we'd watch television. Occasionally, when my mother told me I had had enough, he would give me pocket money. However, dad never gave me a Christmas or birthday present. He never showed me fatherly affection. He never had me as a son.

There were new regulations in the house because of Abel. He kicked Fufi and Panther out of the house as one of his first actions.

"The house is dog-free."

"However, the dogs have always been in the house."

"No longer. Dogs in an African home sleep outdoors. People sleep indoors.

"We're going to do things around here the way they're supposed to be done," Abel said, putting the dogs in the yard. My mother was still the free spirit when they were first dating, traveling where she wanted to go and doing what she wanted. Those things were gradually brought under control. I sensed that he was attempting to control our freedom. He even became agitated over church. He would reply, "You can't spend the entire day at church." "What would people think if my wife is gone all day? Why isn't his wife present? Where is she? Who spends the entire day in church? No, no, no. I feel disrespected by this.

One of his most successful strategies for preventing her from spending so much time at church was to stop repairing my mother's car. He would deliberately let it rest till it broke down. My mom was unable to get the automobile mended elsewhere and could not afford another vehicle. You're going to have your automobile mended by another mechanic even if your spouse is a mechanic? Even worse than cheating is that. As a result, Abel became our sole means of transportation, and he would decline to take us anywhere. My mother, who was always stubborn, would ride minibuses to church.

My dad was likewise unavailable when I lost the automobile. Abel didn't like what they were for, so we had to beg him for a ride into town. It was a slight to his masculinity.

"We must travel to Yeoville."

"What is your reason for visiting Yeoville?"

"To visit Trevor's father."

"What? No, no. How can I drop you off there with my wife and her child? You're making fun of me. What should I say to my pals? What should I say to my family? Is my wife at the home of another man? The man with whom she had that child? No, no, no.

I spent less and less time with my father. He relocated to Cape Town shortly after.

Abel desired a traditional wife and a traditional marriage. My mom was the complete antithesis of that, so I questioned for a long time why dad had ever married her in the first place. Back in Tzaneen, there were plenty of girls being reared just to bow to him if that was what he desired. According to my mother's explanation, a traditional man prefers submissive women, but he never develops feelings for them. He is drawn to self-reliant women. She compared him to a collector of exotic birds. "His dream is to put a woman in a cage, so he only wants a free woman."

Abel was a heavy cannabis user when we first met him. He also drank, but largely marijuana. Because the cannabis calmed him down, I almost miss his pothead days now. He would smoke, relax, watch TV, and then go to sleep. I believe he did it unconsciously because he knew it would help him feel less angry. After he married my mom, he quit smoking. For religious reasons—the body being a temple, etc.—she forced him to stop. However, none of us anticipated that he would simply switch from using marijuana to alcohol. His drinking increased steadily. He was seldom sober when he got home from work. After work, an average day consisted of six beers. He would have a buzz on weeknights. He simply failed to return home on a few Fridays and Saturdays.

Abel's eyes would turn bloodshot red after drinking. I learned to read the clue from it. Abel has always reminded me of a cobra: serene, motionless, and suddenly exploding. No fists were clenched, no yelling and raving. He would be really silent, and then suddenly there would be violence. My sole warning to keep away was the eyes. His eyes were everything. They were the Devil's eyes.

We woke up late one night to a smoke-filled house. By the time we went to bed, Abel hadn't returned home, so I dozed out in my mother's room with her and my infant son Andrew. She was shouting and shaking me as I sprang up. "Trevor! Trevor!" Smoke was all around. We believed the home was on fire.

My mother found the kitchen on fire when she dashed down the hallway to it. Abel had driven home intoxicated, more inebriated than we had ever seen him. He attempted heating up some food on the stove because he was hungry, and while it was cooking, he passed out on the couch. Smoke billowed everywhere, and the pot had burned itself out, destroying the kitchen wall behind the stove. In an attempt to get some fresh air into the room, she shut off the stove and opened the windows and doors. She then roused him up by approaching the couch and began scolding him for almost setting the home on fire. Too inebriated to give a damn.

Returning to the bedroom, she grabbed the phone and dialed my grandmother. She began to talk endlessly about Abel's drinking. "One day, this man will kill us." He nearly set the house on fire.

Abel entered the bedroom in a very quiet and serene manner. His eyelids were thick, and his eyes were blood red. After placing a finger on the cradle, he ended the call. My mother went crazy.

"You dare! Please do not end my call! What are you doing, in your opinion?

He remarked, "You don't tell people what's going on in this house."

"Oh, please! Are you concerned about the opinions of others? Concern yourself with this world! Concern yourself with your family's opinions!

My mother was dwarfed by Abel. He didn't become irate or raise his voice.

He whispered, "Mbuyi, you don't respect me."

"Decency? You nearly set our house on fire. Deference? Oh, please! Get your respect! Act like a man if you want me to regard you as such! Where are your child's diapers, and are you drinking your money on the streets? Show some respect! Get your respect—

"Mbuyi—"

"You are a child, not a man—"

"Mbuyi—"

"I can't have a husband and a child—"

"Mbuyi—"

"I have to raise my own kids—"

"Mbuyi, please stop talking—"

"A man who returns home intoxicated—" "Mbuyi, stop talking—" "and sets the house on fire with his kids—"

"Mbuyi, please stop talking—"

"And you identify as a father—"

He then suddenly slapped her across the face, cracking like a thunderclap in the absence of clouds. She fell like a tonne of bricks after bouncing against the wall. It was unlike anything I had ever seen. She fell and remained down for at least 30 seconds. Andrew began to scream. I distinctly recall holding him at one time, but I don't recall going to pick him up. My mother got back up, stumbled back to her feet, and slammed into him again. She was trying to seem more composed than she actually was, even though it was obvious that she had been taken by surprise. Her expression of disbelief was visible to me. She had never experienced this in her life. She immediately returned to his face and began yelling at him.

"Have you just struck me?"

I was mentally repeating what Abel was saying the entire time. Mom, please stop talking. Quit talking. You will exacerbate the situation. Since I've been beaten a lot, I realized that talking back is the one thing that doesn't help. She wouldn't be silent, though.

"Have you just struck me?"

"I told you—" Mbuyi

"Never has a man! You can't even control—" Don't think you can control me.

Break! He struck her once more. She staggered back but avoided falling this time. She scurried, snatched Andrew and me.

"Come on. We're heading out.

We bolted up the road and out of the house. It was cold outside and it was the dead of night. All I had on was a T-shirt and sweatpants. We walked more than a kilometer to the Eden Park police station. Two police officers were on duty at the front desk as my mother marched us in.

She declared, "I'm here to lay a charge."

"What do you intend to accuse me of?"

"I'm here to accuse the man who struck me of something."

I will always remember the condescending and patronizing manner in which they addressed her.

"Slow down, lady. Relax. Who struck you?

"My spouse."

"Your spouse? What did you do? Did you aggravate him?

Did I—what? No. He struck me. I am here in order to accuse—

"No, no. Ma'am. You want to make a case, but why? Are you certain that you want to do this? Talk to your hubby when you get home. You are aware that once charges are laid, they cannot be withdrawn? There will be a criminal record for him. Nothing will ever be the same in his life. Is your husband's incarceration something you truly want?

They literally refused to type up a charge sheet, despite my mom's persistent demands that they take a statement and file a case.

They declared, "This is a family affair." "You don't want the police to get involved. Perhaps you should reconsider and return in the morning.

Abel entered the station just as Mom began to rage at them, insisting that they see the station commander. He had driven down. Even though he had somewhat sobered up, he was still driving into a police station while intoxicated. That was irrelevant. The station became a boys' club as he approached the police. As though they were old friends.

He said, "Hey, guys." "You are aware of how it is. Women can be, you know. All I did was get a little irate.

"Don't worry, dude. We are aware. It occurs. Do not be concerned.

It was unlike anything I had ever seen. Even at the age of nine, I still believed that the cops were the good ones. while you call the police while you're in difficulty, those red-and-blue lights will come to your aid. However, I recall standing there and watching my mother, shocked and appalled that these police officers refused to assist her. I came to the realization that the police were not who I had assumed they were. First and foremost, they were men, followed by police.

We walked out of the station. Andrew and I were taken by my mother to spend some time with my grandmother in Soweto. Abel drove over and apologized a few weeks later. Abel's apologies were usually genuine and heartfelt: He didn't mean it. He is aware of his error. He won't do it ever again. My mom was persuaded to give Abel another try by my grandmother. "All men do it," was essentially her argument. Temperance, my grandfather, had struck her. Even though Abel was at least prepared to apologize, leaving him did not ensure that it would not happen again. My mother therefore made the decision to give him another chance. We took a car back to Eden Park together, and for years, Abel didn't touch her at all. or myself. Everything returned to its previous state.

Abel was a fantastic technician, arguably among the best in the business at the time. He had attended a technical college and placed top in his class upon graduation. Mercedes and BMW had offered him jobs. Referrals were the lifeblood of his business. He could do miracles on cars, so people would bring them to him from all around the city to be fixed. My mother genuinely had faith in him. She believed she could help him reach his full potential and become the owner of his own workshop in addition to becoming a technician.

Despite her independence and independence, my mother is still the giving woman. It's in her nature to give and give and give. She wanted Abel to be a successful man, but she refused to be obedient to him at home. She was prepared to give her all to their marriage, just as she gave her everything to her children, if she could make it a true marriage of equals. Abel's boss eventually made the decision to retire and sell Mighty Mechanics. Abel was assisted in purchasing it by my mom, who had some money put up. Mighty Mechanics became the new family business after they relocated the workshop from Yeoville to the industrial region of Wynberg, which is located just west of Alex.

There are a lot of things no one tells you when you first start your own business. That's particularly true if you're two young Black individuals—a mechanic and a secretary—coming from an era when black people were not permitted to own any kind of business. When you purchase a firm, you also purchase its debt, which is one of the things no one tells you. The corporation was already in a lot of trouble when my mom and Abel opened the Mighty Mechanics books and realized what they had purchased.

Our lives were progressively overtaken by the garage. After school, I would travel the five kilometers to the workshop from Maryvale. With all of the equipment and repairs going on around me, I would sit for hours trying to finish my homework. Since Abel was our ride, we would have to wait for him to complete before we could leave for home because he would inevitably get behind time. "We're running late," was the initial statement. We'll let you know when we're leaving, so go take a nap in the car. We would drive all the way back out to Eden Park and crash after they woke me up at midnight and I crawled in the backseat of some sedan. Soon after, it was "We're running late." We'll wake you up for school in the morning, so go sleep in a car. We went to the garage to sleep. One or two nights a week at first, then three or four. After that, my mother sold the house and used the proceeds to fund the business. She gave it her all. For him, she sacrificed everything.

We moved into the garage and lived there ever since. In essence, it was a warehouse—not the posh, romantic kind that hipsters might eventually convert into lofts. No, no. The room was chilly and deserted. There are old trash automobiles and auto parts all over the place, and the gray concrete flooring are soiled with oil and grease. There was a little drywall office for handling documents and other things next to the entrance, next to the roller door that led onto the street. A kitchenette with a sink, a portable hot plate, and a few cabinets was located in the back. All that was available for bathing was an open wash basin with a showerhead installed above, like a janitor's sink.

In the workplace, Abel, my mother, and Andrew slept on a tiny mattress that they would spread out on the floor. I slept in the automobiles. I became rather skilled at dozing off in automobiles. I am aware of all the top cars for sleeping in. Volkswagens and low-end Japanese sedans were the worst. Cheap faux-leather upholstery, no headrests, and barely reclined chairs. I would try not to slide off the seat for half of the night. I was unable to stretch and extend my legs, so I would wake up with painful knees. German automobiles, particularly Mercedes, were fantastic. Large, luxurious leather seats that resemble couches. When you initially climbed in, they were chilly, but they were warm and well-insulated. I could get pretty warm inside a Mercedes with just my school blazer to wrap up under. However, American automobiles were by far the greatest. I used to hope and pray that a customer would arrive with a large Buick that had bench seats. I would say "yes" if I saw one of those! American automobiles were infrequently, but when they were, I was ecstatic.

I had to work since I was family and Mighty Mechanics was now a family business. Play was out of the question. Even homework was out of the question. I would put on my overalls, take off my school uniform, stroll home, and climb under the hood of a car. I eventually became capable of performing a basic auto repair on my own, which I frequently did. "That Honda," Abel would say. minor service. I would also go beneath the hood. day in and day out. air filters, oil filters, condensers, plugs, and points. Replace the headlights, replace the tires, install new seats, and fix the taillights. Proceed to the parts store, make your purchase, and then return to the workshop. That was my life at the age of eleven. I was slipping academically. I wasn't accomplishing anything. My instructors used to be critical of me.

"What's stopping you from doing your homework?"

I'm unable to complete my schoolwork. I'm working from home.

We put in endless hours, but the business continued to lose money despite our efforts. Everything was lost. Real food was out of our price range. The hardest month of my life was one that I will never forget. For weeks, we only ate bowls of marogo, a type of wild spinach fried with caterpillars, because we were so poor. We call them mopane worms. Only the lowest of the impoverished consume mopane worms, which are literally the cheapest food. I was raised in poverty, but there are two extremes: poverty and "Wait, I'm eating worms." Even people in Soweto would say, "Eh...no," when they saw mopane worms. These are finger-sized, spiky, vibrantly colored caterpillars. They are not comparable to escargot, which is a snail that has been given a fancy name. What filthy worms they are. As you chew them, the black spines on them prickle the roof of your mouth. The yellow-green excrement of mopane worms frequently squirts into your mouth when you bite into one.

For a while, I kind of liked the caterpillars. I finally lost patience after eating them daily for weeks. It resembled embarking on a culinary adventure. The day I chewed a mopane worm in half and watched the yellow-green slime that came out made me think, "I'm eating caterpillar shit," and I will never forget it. I immediately wanted to throw up. I raced to my mother and broke down in tears. "I want to stop eating caterpillars!" That night, she was able to get some money together and buy us some chicken. Although we had been poor before, we had never been without food.

Working through the night, sleeping in a car, waking up, washing in a janitor's sink, brushing my teeth in a tiny metal basin, brushing my hair in the rearview mirror of a Toyota, and then trying to get dressed without getting oil and grease on my school clothes so the kids wouldn't know I lived in a garage—that was the period of my life that I hated the most. I hated it so much. I hated cars. Sleeping in cars was something I hated. Auto repair was something I hated to do. It was something I hated to get dirty. I didn't like eating worms. I hated everything.

It's funny because I saw how hard everyone was working, so I didn't hate my mother or even Abel. At first, it seemed like a challenging situation because I was not aware of the business-level mistakes making it thus. But eventually, I started to see why the business was losing money. When I used to go around and acquire Abel his car components, I found out that he was buying them on credit. The dealers were charging him a ridiculous markup. The firm was being destroyed because he was drinking the little money he made instead of repaying the debt. A great technician but a bad businessman.

I endured a lot of my mother's traditional, Old Testament discipline as a child. She didn't spoil any kids or spare any rods. She was not the same with Andrew. Initially, he received spankings, but they gradually decreased and then stopped. She joked about it, as she often does, when I asked why Andrew didn't get a thrashing when I did. She remarked, "I beat you that way because you could handle it." "Your younger brother is a tiny little stick, so I can't whack him the same way. He will shatter. However, God gave you that ass to beat. She may have been joking, but I could tell that she had a sincere change of heart, which is why she didn't beat Andrew. She had, strangely enough, learned that lesson from me.

Despite growing up in a violent environment, I was never aggressive myself. I did break windows, start fires, and pull practical jokes, but I never attacked anyone. I don't ever hit anybody. I was never upset. That's just not how I saw myself. The world my mother had grown up in was not the same as the one she had shown me. She never got around to reading the books she purchased me. She showed me the schools she was never able to visit. I lost myself in those universes and returned with a new perspective on the world. I discovered that not every family is violent. I witnessed the pointlessness of violence, the never-ending cycle, and the harm done to those who then harm others.

More than anything, I realized that love, not violence, is what keeps partnerships going. The act of love is creative. You make a whole new world for someone you love. My mother did that for me, and I returned with a new world and a new understanding for her based on my growth and new knowledge. She never again raised her hand to her children after that. Unfortunately, Abel had already begun when she stopped.

Despite all of the times my mother hit me, I never felt afraid of her. Of course I didn't like it. I wasn't necessarily in agreement with her reasoning when she claimed, "I hit you out of love." However, I realized that it was discipline and that there was a reason for it. I experienced a sensation I had never experienced before when Abel struck me. I was terrified.

In my final year at Maryvale, I was in grade six. After we relocated to Highlands North, I got in trouble at school for using my mother's name to sign a document. I signed the release in her name to avoid being involved in an activity I didn't want to be a part of. When I arrived home that afternoon, my mother, who had been contacted by the school, asked me about it. This was one of those occasions when she didn't care, even though I was positive she would punish me. She stated she would have signed the form anyhow, so I should have just asked. "Hey, can I talk to you for a second?" remarked Abel, who had been watching the entire event from the kitchen. He then led me into this small space, which was a walk-in pantry off the kitchen, and shut the door after us.

I didn't give his presence between me and the door any thought. I didn't think I should be afraid. I had never been disciplined by Abel before. I had never even received a lecture from him. My mother would deal with it after saying, "Mbuyi, your son did this." It was mid-afternoon at this point. What followed was all the more horrifying since he was totally sober.

He asked, "What made you forge your mother's signature?"

I began to invent an excuse. "Oh, I guess I should have brought the form home—"

"Don't tell me lies. You forged your mother's signature, but why?

Unaware of what was about to happen, I began stuttering out more garbage, and then it suddenly came.

I was struck in the ribs by the initial blow. I thought, "It's a trap!" Despite the fact that I had never engaged in combat before and had never learned how to fight, I felt compelled to approach. I had witnessed the might of those long arms. I had witnessed him defeat my mother, but more significantly, I had witnessed him defeat adult males. Abel never punched anyone, and I never witnessed him use a closed hand to strike someone. However, he had the power to crumple a grown man by striking him across the face with an open palm. He was that powerful. Don't be on the receiving end of those things, I understood after glancing at his arms. He continued to strike as I dodged in close, but I was too close for him to deliver any serious hits. After he realized what was going on, he stopped striking and began attempting to wrestle me. He gripped the skin on my arms, pinched it between his thumb and fingers, and then twisted violently. That stung, Jesus.

It was the scariest thing I have ever experienced. Never in my life had I been so afraid. The reason it was so terrible was that it had no purpose. Discipline wasn't the issue. It wasn't coming from a loving place at all. I didn't think I would learn a lesson about faking my mother's signature at the end of it. It seemed to finish when he wanted it to, when he had had enough of his anger. He had a feeling that something inside of him wanted to ruin me.

Even though Abel was considerably larger and stronger than me, I benefited from being in a small area since he had less space to move about. I somehow twisted and wriggled my way around him and slipped out the door as he struggled and punched. Not only was I fast, but so was Abel. He came after me. After leaving the home, I sprang over the gate and continued to run. When I last turned around, he was coming out of the yard after me, rounding the gate. The expression on his face as he turned the corner was a recurrent nightmare of mine until I was twenty-five.

I dropped my head and started running as soon as I spotted him. I ran as if I were being pursued by the Devil. This was my neighborhood, but Abel was bigger and faster. You couldn't find me in my community. I was familiar with every street and alley, every wall to scale, and every fence to get past. I was cutting across yards and dodging vehicles. I never looked back, so I don't know when he gave up. I continued to run as far as my legs would allow. Before I stopped, I was three neighborhoods away in Bramley. I crouched for what seemed like hours after finding a hiding spot in some bushes and crawling inside.

I don't need a second lesson from you. I stayed in that house like a mouse from that day till the day I moved out. I stayed out of any room where Abel was present. I was in one corner if he was in another. I would get up and pretend to go to the kitchen if he entered a room, and then I would make sure I was near the exit when I returned. He might be in his most joyful, amiable state. didn't matter. I never allowed him to get in the way of a door again. After that, I might have been careless a few times and he would punch or kick me before I could escape, but I never again trusted him.

For Andrew, it was different. Andrew's flesh and blood were those of Abel's son. Andrew was actually Abel's firstborn son and the oldest son in that household, which gave him a respect that neither my mother nor I ever experienced, even though he was nine years younger than me. And in spite of his flaws, Andrew loved that man unconditionally. I believe that Andrew was the only one among us who wasn't terrified because of his love. He was the lion tamer, but because he had grown up with the lion, he was unable to love the animal any less in spite of its potential. For me, Abel and I had lost the initial flash of rage or insanity. Staying, Andrew would attempt to calm Abel down. He would even stand between Mom and Abel. Abel tossed a bottle of Jack Daniel's at Andrew's head one evening, as I recall. It exploded on the wall, almost missing him. In other words, Andrew lingered long enough to receive the bottle. Abel couldn't have gotten a bead on me if I had lingered.

Abel had to remove his vehicles when Mighty Mechanics went down. Liens were placed on his assets, and someone was occupying the property. It was a complete disaster. At that point, he began using our yard as his workshop. Additionally, my mother divorced him at that time.

One of the neighbors petitioned to have us removed because Abel had begun operating an unlicensed business in a residential neighborhood. In order to run a company on the property, my mom sought for a license. Abel continued to drink his money while running the workshop into the ground. My mother began advancing in her career at the real estate firm she worked for at the same time, assuming greater responsibility and receiving a higher salary. His craft practically turned into a side pastime. He was expected to cover Andrew's groceries and school fees, but he began to lag behind even on those, and before long, my mom was covering everything. She covered the cost of the energy. She made the mortgage payment. He made absolutely no contribution.

That was the pivotal moment. The dragon appeared when my mother began earning more money and regaining her freedom. The drinking worsened. He became increasingly aggressive. Abel struck my mother for the second time shortly after he came for me in the pantry. Because it is now mixed up with all the other occasions that followed it, I am unable to remember the specifics of it. The police were summoned, I do recall. Once more, it felt like a guys' club as they came out to the house. "Hey everyone. You are aware of the nature of these women. There was no report. There were no charges brought.

My mother would find me crying after he hit her or chased me and pull me away. Every time, she would give me the same speech.

"Support Abel," she would urge. "Because he is not hostile toward us." He despises himself.

This is incomprehensible to a child. "Well, why doesn't he kick himself if he hates himself?" I would ask.

Abel was one of those drinkers who, after he left, you couldn't even see the same person when you looked into his eyes. One night, I recall, he came home intoxicated and staggered around the house. I woke up to watch him pull out his dick and begin urinating on the floor after he staggered into my room while cursing to himself. He believed that he was in the restroom. He would become so inebriated that he would lose his sense of which part of the house he was in. He would frequently enter my room by mistake, believing it to be his, kick me out of bed, and faint. It felt like I was speaking to a zombie when I screamed at him. I would take a nap on the couch.

Every night after work, he would get intoxicated with his group in the backyard, and on many occasions, he would wind up fighting with one of them. Abel would beat the living daylights out of him whenever someone said something that he didn't like. The man would be absent from work on Tuesdays and Wednesdays, but he would return by Thursday since he had to do the job. Like clockwork, the same story was told every few weeks.

Abel also kicked the dogs. Mostly fufi. The lovely but stupid Fufi was constantly attempting to be Abel's friend, but Panther was wise enough to avoid him. When he had had enough, he would eject her if she crossed his route or got in his way. She would then leave and spend some time hiding somewhere. When a fufi got kicked, it was always an indication that something bad was going to happen. The rest of us knew to keep quiet because the dogs and the yard workers frequently had the first taste of his rage. Normally, I would go locate Fufi and stay with her wherever she was hiding.

The odd thing was that Fufi never screamed or yelled when she was kicked. In addition to diagnosing her as deaf, the veterinarian discovered that she had a disease that prevented her sense of touch from developing fully. She was painless. She would therefore constantly begin anew with Abel as if it were the first time. She would hide when he kicked her, but she would return the following morning, wagging her tail. "Hey. I'm present. I'll give you another opportunity.

And he was always given another chance. There was always that likeable, affable Abel. He was a kind man, but he had a drinking problem. We were a family. You struggle with the idea that you can love someone you hate or hate someone you love if you were raised in an abusive household. It's an odd sensation. You wish to live in a world where people are either nice or bad, and you either love or detest them, but that isn't the reality.

Although there was a general feeling of fear in the house, the beatings themselves did not happen very often. I believe that things would have been resolved sooner if they had been. Ironically, it was the enjoyable moments in between that made it possible for it to drag on and intensify to this extent. After hitting my mom once, he did it again three years later, this time with somewhat more force. When it happened two years later, it was slightly worse. However, a year later, things were slightly worse. It was often enough that you never forgot it was conceivable, yet it was infrequent enough that you would think it wouldn't happen again. Something had a beat to it. I recall that for more than a month, no one spoke to him following a horrible tragedy. Nothing—no dialogue, no eye contact, no words. At separate occasions, we passed through the house as strangers. total silence. One morning, you're in the kitchen when someone nods. "Hi." "Hi." "Did you see the thing on the news?" is the question that follows a week later. "Yes." The following week, there is a laugh and a joke. Life gradually returns to its former state. You repeat the entire process six months or a year later.

When I got home from Sandringham one day, my mother was agitated and upset.

She remarked, "This man is unbelievable."

"What took place?"

"He purchased a firearm."

"What? A firearm? "He bought a gun," what do you mean?

In my world, a gun was absolutely absurd. I thought weapons were only for police officers and criminals. Abel had gone out and purchased a Smith & Wesson Parabellum 9mm. ominous, dark and sleek. Compared to guns in movies, it didn't look cool. It appeared to have killed things.

I questioned, "Why did he purchase a firearm?"

"I'm not sure."

She claimed that when she challenged him about it, he went out on a tirade about how everyone should respect him.

She remarked, "He believes he is the world's best police officer." And that is the world's dilemma. Some people desire to police everyone around them because they are unable to police themselves.

I moved out shortly after that. For me, the atmosphere had turned poisonous. By this time, I had grown to Abel's size. Large enough to retaliate. I was not a parent's son, but a father does not fear his son's vengeance. He was aware of that. My mother compared it like having two male lions in the house today. She would say, "He sees your father every time he looks at you." "You remind me of another man all the time. You must go; he despises you. You must depart before you turn into him.

After a while, my mom moved into a different bedroom in the house, and they were legally married but merely lived together. That situation persisted for a year or possibly two. I was counting down the days until Andrew reached eighteen because I thought that would finally release my mom from this horrible man. Andrew had turned nine. My mother then called me one afternoon and invited me to stop by the house. I stopped by after a few of hours.

"Trevor," she said. "I am expecting a child."

"What, I'm sorry?"

"I am expecting a child."

"What?"

My goodness, I was angry. I was furious. She appeared resolute, as determined as ever, but with a melancholy I had never seen before, as if the news had initially devastated her but that she had already come to terms with it.

"How could you have allowed this to occur?"

"I made up with Abel. I returned to the bedroom. After only a single night, I became pregnant. I have no idea how.

She was unaware. Fourty-four was her age. After Andrew, she had her tubes tied. This shouldn't be feasible, even according to her doctor. We have no idea how this occurred.

My anger was boiling over. It seemed as though she had renewed the contract, and all we needed to do was wait for Andrew to mature.

"So, you and this man are going to have a child? Are you planning to spend another eighteen years with this man? Are you insane?

"I heard from God, Trevor. "Patricia," he assured me, "I never do anything by accident." Nothing I give you is too much for you to bear. There's a reason I'm pregnant. I am aware of the type of children I can produce. I am aware of the type of sons I can bring up. This child can be raised by me. This child will be raised by me.

Isaac was born nine months after that. She gave him the name Isaac because, according to the Bible, Sarah becomes pregnant at the age of 100, when she shouldn't be having children, and she names her son after him.

The birth of Isaac made me even more distant. I went less and less. The house was in disarray when I visited one afternoon, with police cars outside and the aftermath of yet another altercation.

He would use a bicycle to strike her. My mother had attempted to intervene when Abel was reprimanding one of his employees in the yard. Abel grabbed Andrew's bike and beat her with it because he was upset that she had lied to him in front of a coworker. She contacted the police once more, and this time the officers who arrived knew Abel. Their autos were fixed by him. They were friends. There were no charges brought. Nothing took place.

I challenged him at that moment. Now I was large enough.

I said, "You can't continue doing this." "This is incorrect."

He expressed regret. He was always. He didn't become defensive, push out his chest, or do anything similar.

"I understand," he said. "I apologize. Although I dislike doing these things, you are aware of your mother's nature. She doesn't listen and can talk a lot. Sometimes I think your mother doesn't respect me. In front of my employees, she arrived and treated me disrespectfully. These other men can't be staring at me as if I'm incapable of managing my wife.

After the bicycle, my mom moved in with Isaac and hired contractors she knew from the real estate industry to build her a separate house in the backyard that resembled tiny servant quarters.

I told her, "This is the most crazy thing I've ever seen."

"This is my only option," she declared. "I can't get aid from the cops. I will not be protected by the government. I can only be protected by my God. However, I have the ability to use his pride—the one thing he values—against him. Everyone will ask him, "Why does your wife live in a shack outside your house?" because I live outside in a shack. He will have to respond to that question, and regardless of his response, everyone will be aware that he is flawed. He enjoys living life to the fullest. Give the world a glimpse of his true self. In the streets, he is a saint. In this household, he is a devil. Allow him to be recognized for who he is.

I was on the verge of dismissing my mother when she made the decision to keep Isaac. The agony became unbearable to me. The last straw for me, though, was witnessing her get struck by a bicycle and living like a prisoner in her own backyard. I was a damaged individual. I was finished.

I said to her, "This thing?" "This broken thing? I will not participate in it. I cannot coexist with you in this world. I decline. You've already decided. I wish you luck in life. My life will be mine.

She got it. She had no sense of abandonment or betrayal.

She said, "Honey, I understand what you're going through." I had to leave my family at one time in order to start living my own life. I can see why you must follow suit.

So I did. I left. I did not make a call. I didn't go. I left after Isaac arrived, and I couldn't for the life of me figure out why she wouldn't follow suit. Simply go. Just fuck off.

I had no idea what she was dealing with. I had no idea what domestic violence was. I had never even had a girlfriend, so I had no idea how mature relationships operated. How she could have sex with a man she feared and detested was beyond me. I had never idea how readily fear, hatred, and sex could converge.

I felt resentful of my mother. I blamed her even though I detested him. In my opinion, Abel was a decision she had made and was still making. She had always told me stories of her upbringing in the homelands and her parents' abandonment, and she always remarked, "You cannot blame anyone else for what you do." Your identity cannot be attributed to your past. You are in charge of yourself. You are the one who makes your own decisions.

I never saw us as victims because of her. Andrew, Isaac, my mother, and I were all victims. prisoners of apartheid. abuse victims. I didn't perceive her life that way, though, and I was never permitted to think that way. She made the decision to remove my father from our lives in order to appease Abel. She decided to support Abel's workshop. She chose Isaac. He didn't have the money; she did. She wasn't reliant. I therefore believed that she was the one who made the choice.

Putting the blame on the woman and telling her to go is so simple from the outside. It's not as though domestic violence was unique to my household. I grew up surrounded by it. I saw it on TV, in movies, and in the streets of Soweto. In a culture where such is the standard, where does a woman go? When the police refuse to assist her? When her own relatives refuse to assist her? When a woman leaves a man who abuses her and is as likely to end up with another man who abuses her, possibly even more severely than the first, where does she go? When a lady has three children and is single, living in a culture that stigmatizes her for being a woman without a partner, where does she go? For doing that, is she viewed as a whore? Where does she go? What is she doing?

However, at the time, I didn't understand any of it. I had a boy's perspective on the world when I was a boy. I also vividly recall our most recent argument over it. It was either when she was relocating to her backyard shack or after the bicycle. For the thousandth time, I was pleading with her as I left.

"Why? Why don't you simply go?

She gave a headshake. "Oh, sweetheart. No, no, no. I am unable to go.

"Why not?"

"Because he will kill us if I leave."

She was not acting fanciful. She didn't speak louder. I never asked her the question again after she answered it in a very composed and matter-of-fact manner.

She did eventually depart. I'm not sure what caused her to leave or what the last straw was. I had left. I was traveling the country, performing in England, doing radio shows, and hosting television shows as a comic. I had separated my life from my cousin Mlungisi's after moving in with her. Since it would have split me into too many pieces, I was no longer able to invest myself. However, she eventually met someone new, bought a new home in Highlands North, and moved on with her life. Andrew and Isaac continued to see their father, who by that time was only surviving, still engaging in the same pattern of drinking and arguing, and still residing in a home that his ex-wife had paid for.

Years went by. Life continued.

Then, one morning at around eleven in the morning, my phone called when I was in bed. It happened on a Sunday. The irony of my life is that bad things always happen when church is involved, such as when aggressive minibus drivers kidnap people. I had also always made fun of my mother for that. "What good has come of all this Jesus, this church thing of yours?"

I turned to face my phone. When I responded, Andrew was on the other end, even though it was showing my mom's number. He sounded completely composed.

"Hi Trevor, this is Andrew."

"Hi."

"How are you?"

"All right. What's going on?

"Are you occupied?"

"I'm sleeping, sort of. Why?

"Mom was shot."

Alright, so the call had two peculiar aspects. To begin with, why would he inquire as to my busyness? Let's begin there. "Mom's been shot" should be the first thing you say after your mother is shot. Not "How are you?" Not "Are you busy?" I was perplexed by that. The second strange thing was that I didn't inquire, "Who shot Mom?" when he responded, "Mom's been shot." I didn't have to. My mind quickly filled in the rest when he said, "Mom's been shot": "Abel shot mom."

"Now, where are you?" "I said."

"Linksfield Hospital is our location."

"All right, I'm headed out."

My body simply released itself when he uttered that. I can still clearly recall the precise traffic light I was at. There was an absolute silence for a time, and then I started crying as I had never sobbed before. I broke out in heavy groans and tears. I sobbed as though all the other things I had ever cried for had been pointless. I sobbed so much that my current crying self would slap my previous crying selves and tell them, "That shit isn't worth crying for," if it could travel back in time and witness them. I didn't cry out of grief. Catharsis was not what it was. I wasn't apologizing for myself. It was an outburst of unadulterated pain that resulted from my body's incapacity to communicate that pain in any other manner. She was my mother. She was a member of my team. I had always been with her, and we had always been against the world. I split in two when Andrew stated, "shot her in the head."

I spun around and dashed into the emergency department. My mother was on a gurney in triage. She was being stabilized by the doctors. The blood was all over her body. She had lost a portion of her nose, a hole in her face, and a wide cut above her lip.

I had never seen her so placid and at ease. She was still able to open one eye, and she turned to face me after noticing my horrified expression.

With blood in her throat, she could hardly talk, but she muttered, "It's okay, baby."

"It's not acceptable."

"No, no, I'm all right. Andrew, where are you? Where is your brother?

"He's out there."

"Go see Andrew."

"But, Mom—"

"Shhh. It's all right, sweetie. I'm all right.

"You aren't okay, you're—"

"Shhhhhh. I'm all right, all OK. Visit your brother. You are needed by your sibling.

He claimed that the bullet that struck my mother in the butt was a through-and-through. It entered, exited, and caused no actual harm. The other bullet entered near the top of her neck, below the skull, and passed through the back of her head. It passed through her head just below the brain, missing all of the main veins, arteries, and nerves, and just missed the spinal cord and medulla oblongata. The bullet would have blown out her eye due to its trajectory, which was aimed directly for her left eye socket. However, it slowed down at the last second, struck her cheekbone instead, broke it, bounced off, and exited via her left nostril. The blood had made the wound appear much worse than it was on the gurney in the emergency room. It came out clean, with no bullet parts remaining within, and the bullet merely removed a small flap of flesh on the side of her nostril. Surgery wasn't even necessary for her. She was sewed up in front and back, the bleeding was stopped, and she was allowed to heal.

The doctor stated, "There was nothing we can do, because there is nothing we need to do."

Within four days, my mother was discharged from the hospital. At seven o'clock, she returned to her job.

For the remainder of the day and night, the physicians kept her drugged so she could rest. We were all told to return home. They declared, "She is stable." "You have nothing to do in this situation. Return home and rest. So we did.

The following morning, I returned right away to wait for my mother to wake up in her bed. She was still asleep when I entered. She had bandages on the back of her head. Her nose and left eye were covered in gauze, and she had sutures in her face. It was one of the few occasions in my life that I had ever seen her appear so weak and exhausted.

A flurry of ideas raced through my head as I sat near her bed, holding her hand, waiting, and watching her breathe. I continued to worry that I might lose her. I was upset with the cops for not arresting Abel and with myself for not being present. Although it was absurd to suppose that I should have murdered him years ago because I am incapable of murdering anyone, I did it nevertheless. I was upset with God and the world. since my mother only prays. My mom is undoubtedly among the top 100 members of any fan club for Jesus, and this is what she receives?

She waited for about an hour before opening her unbandaged eye. I lost it the moment she did. I began to cry. I offered her a cup of water when she asked for it, and she leaned forward slightly to take a sip via the straw. I continued to cry uncontrollably. I was unable to restrain myself.

"Shh," she said. "Baby, don't cry. Shhhh. Don't cry."

"Mom, how am I not crying? You nearly lost your life.

"No, I was not going to pass away. I had no intention of dying. It's all right. I had no intention of dying.

"But I believed you had passed away." I wept uncontrollably. "I believed I had lost you."

"No, sweetheart. Don't cry, baby. Trevor. Listen, Trevor. Pay attention to me. Pay attention.

"What?" With tears running down my cheeks, I spoke.

"You have to see the bright side, my child."

"What? What do you mean when you say "the bright side"? You got shot in the face, Mom. There's nothing positive about it.

"There is, of course. You are now formally the family's most attractive member.

She smiled broadly and burst out laughing. I also started giggling through my tears. I was simultaneously laughing hysterically and crying uncontrollably. On a bright, sunny, and lovely day, we sat there, she gripped my hand, and we laughed together as usual—mother and son, laughing despite the pain in an intensive care unit.

Printed in Great Britain
by Amazon

62988471R00107